CW01507440

DROWNING
LIFEGUARDS

Your Guide to Overcoming
Fatigue, Burnout and Overwhelm

RUTH HULL

This book is intended for general educational purposes only. It is not a substitute for professional medical advice, diagnosis, or treatment. Always consult a qualified health professional before making any changes to your health, lifestyle, or treatment plan. The author and publisher accept no liability for any loss, damage, or injury caused by the use or misuse of the information contained herein.

Copyright © 2025 Ruth Hull

All rights reserved.

No part of this publication may be reproduced, stored in a retrieval system, or transmitted in any form or by any means - electronic, mechanical, photocopying, recording, or otherwise - without prior written permission from the publisher, except for brief quotations used in reviews or articles.

For permissions, contact:

www.ruthhull.com

Cover design by: Sophia Hull

ISBN: 9798289560094

First published in 2025

Printed by Amazon KDP

To my husband, who taught me how to
swim in a sea of overwhelm.

ALSO BY RUTH HULL

...

The Pocket Atlas of Anatomy & Physiology

Anatomy, Physiology and Pathology

Anatomy, Physiology and Pathology Colouring & Workbook

The Complete Guide to Reflexology

The Complete Guide to Reflexology Colouring & Workbook

TABLE OF CONTENTS

INTRODUCTION

"A drowning lifeguard is a lousy lifeguard"
- Seth Godin

Sometimes things seem to fall out of the sky and just hit us on the head. That's how I came across the title for this book: Drowning Lifeguards. I was driving down the freeway one day listening to a podcast in which Seth Godin said: "a drowning lifeguard is a lousy lifeguard."

I work with drowning lifeguards every day. I was one myself for many years.

To me a drowning lifeguard is one of those people who is always helping other people, always putting the needs of their kids, their partners, their work (and anyone and anything else) before their own.

There's nothing wrong with being like this, until you run out of energy and can no longer keep your head above water.

There's nothing wrong with trying to help other people, as long as you've got the energy to keep swimming yourself.

But when you run out of energy, when you start to drown in that sea of overwhelm, who can you help?

You can't help other people, you can't be there emotionally for your kids, and you can't be there energetically for your friends or partner when all you want to do is crawl into bed at 8pm every night and shut the world outside.

Interestingly, most of the drowning lifeguards I've worked with were never really taught to swim.

Some of them didn't grow up with role models or teachers to show them how. Others were thrown in at the deep end and just had to start swimming, with no one there to throw them a rope when they needed it.

Most of them feel lost, alone and unsupported.

If you feel like you're drowning, if you're not really coping with what everyone around you seems to cope with so easily, and you know that this exhausted, tired, overwhelmed, overwrought, grumpy, snapping, tearful, empty shell of a person that you've become isn't really you, then this is the book for you.

It's a step-by-step manual that will teach you how to swim downstream with the current, not upstream battling against everything.

1, THE TIREDNESS THAT WON'T GO AWAY

This book is about fatigue, something everyone experiences from time to time. For most people, fatigue is a state or feeling of extreme tiredness, usually caused by overwork and improved by rest.

For some of us, fatigue is so much more than that. No amount of rest or sleep helps. Fatigue is no longer a passing feeling. It's something that's taken over our lives. Something that affects every facet of who we are and what we do. You could almost call it a beast inside of you.

Or you could call it a teacher.

When I was 19, my gran gave me a book called *Radical Healing* by Rudolph Ballentine. That book inspired me to become a health professional and has shaped much of my life's work. In it, Ballentine shares a story about a psychiatric patient:

"When I first began my training in psychiatry, I was assigned a very disturbed patient who had just been admitted to the locked ward. I prescribed the customary drug, one similar to that still used today in such situations. To my delight, the patient calmed down and seemed remarkably less agitated.

'You seem a lot better!' I enthused the next day.

She studied my face for a moment. 'Not really,' she said. 'Before, I was nervous on the outside. Now I'm nervous on the inside.'"

This story has stuck with me my whole life. It's a constant reminder not to silence or suppress our symptoms too quickly. Every sign and symptom our bodies throw out, every illness or dysfunction, is there for a reason. They're messages. They're trying to tell us something.

What is your fatigue trying to tell you?

I've been practising, teaching and writing about health for 25 years now. Yet it was only through burning myself out that I truly started to understand and integrate what being healthy is all about. The word heal comes from the Old English word *hāl*, meaning whole, and being healthy is about feeling as if you are whole exactly as you are. It's about accepting yourself as you are, right now. It's about integrating everything you've been through in life and recognising your wholeness despite your wounds and scars.

Healing isn't about fixing, curing or changing yourself. It's not about ignoring or removing the parts of you that you don't like. If you feel broken, you can't feel whole. If you ignore or suppress a part of who you are, you can't feel whole. As Eckhart Tolle said, "What could be more futile, more insane, than to create inner resistance to what already is?"

The purpose of this book is to guide you to create time and space in your life to explore who you are and what health and energy mean to you. I hope to give you the tools to do this so that you can discover what I believe is the truth behind all healing: that everything you need is already inside of you.

WHY ARE YOU SO TIRED?

When I look back at my patients with fatigue, not one of them has been a lazy couch-potato watching TV all day. In fact, they've all been hard workers and high achievers. And something more - they've been the givers in relationships, the carers, the ones who are always there when someone needs them.

7

I've also noticed a much deeper pattern that may be best explained through some questions.

These questions may be a little challenging, but they come without judgment or blame and are curious questions that may help spark something inside you:

- As a child, did you have to grow up quickly because of illness, addiction, or emotional chaos in your family? Were you responsible for the happiness or safety of other people from a young age?
- When you were young were you forced to do things completely against your will? Do you have things you have to hide even from the people closest to you? Do you carry secrets or burdens you cannot share?
- Have you lived through deep shock or loss such as the death of a loved one, the loss of your home, country, or sense of safety?
- Have you lived for years with an ongoing stress such as chronic pain, illness, financial stress, or caring for someone else?
- Essentially, do you feel out of control, powerless? As if someone, or something, has ripped the rug out from under your feet, and you've never quite got your footing back.

I haven't asked whether you work too hard. I believe overwork is a symptom of something deeper and the real question is not why are you so tired, but why are you pushing yourself so hard? Why aren't you listening to your body? Why aren't you being gentler with yourself?

Tiredness isn't a flaw in who you are. It's a response to what you've been through. Life has thrown you off balance.

IS IT ALL IN YOUR HEAD?

Do you sometimes wonder if you're making this whole "fatigue" thing up? If maybe there's really nothing wrong with you and you're just tired like everyone else these days. Or maybe, like many of my patients, you've been to your doctor, had all the tests, been told nothing's wrong and probably prescribed antidepressants.

The thing with fatigue is that it's accompanied with other symptoms we hardly notice. I'm not sure if we don't notice them because we're so tired, or if these symptoms creep up on us so slowly and quietly that we get used to them and think they're normal.

Even as a health professional, I didn't question the strange symptoms showing up in my body when I was burned out. I was in my early thirties, having night sweats most nights, fainting regularly and losing my breath when walking up a short flight of stairs. I dismissed it all. It didn't occur to me that those symptoms were my body trying to tell me something.

A QUICK CHECK-IN

Before you keep reading, take a moment to check in with yourself. The list below includes some common signs of deep fatigue. Go through them and highlight anything that feels familiar - not to diagnose, but simply to notice. This is your body's way of speaking to you.

- o Common signs of fatigue include:
- o Sore throat
- o Frequent infections (coughs, colds, tonsillitis)
- o Sore muscles, tight neck and shoulders
- o Backache or joint pain
- o Headaches or migraines
- o Brain fog, poor concentration, forgetfulness

o Food intolerances
o Skin rashes, eczema, or hives
o Hay fever, postnasal drip, or sinusitis
o Fatigue and pain after exercising.

These symptoms may be common, but they're not normal and they're certainly not imaginary.

More importantly, they're warning signs. I've seen time and again that people who keep pushing through despite these early messages often go on to develop more complex, long-term conditions like:

o Low blood pressure
o Insomnia
o Night sweats
o Low testosterone
o Period (ovulation) problems
o Thyroid issues
o Heart problems
o Autoimmune disease.

I'm writing this book to help you unpack the layers of your fatigue so you can start rebuilding your health physically, emotionally, and energetically. You'll find step-by-step guidance on everything from food and sleep to emotional healing and deeper self-awareness.

I'll be asking you to do quite a lot of 'work' as you go through. You'll be reflecting, taking notes, tracking symptoms, and gently exploring parts of yourself that might need attention so I recommend keeping a journal or notebook nearby as you read. Let it be a space to make sense of what you're feeling, record changes, and track your healing journey over time.

There are many dimensions to fatigue and it's often so quiet and insidious that we live with it for years before realising something's wrong. Then, too often we try to treat it as one thing or the other - physical or emotional. Yet in truth, the two are deeply connected. One affects the other. You can't untangle them. As Plato once said, "The greatest mistake in the treatment of disease is that there are physicians for the body and physicians for the soul, although the two cannot be separated."

I didn't fully understand just how connected the physical and emotional were until one of my reflexology clients came into my clinic, exploding with frustration.

I hadn't seen her for a while, but she had previously come to me for about a year. In the beginning, she barely spoke. She was small, tense and tightly wound, and had originally booked in because of depression. Everything about her felt hard and guarded. But she kept showing up, week after week, and gradually started to open up.

One day, she told me she believed her husband was having an affair. She'd suspected it for years but had never confronted him. She'd kept everything bottled up, pretending nothing was wrong. It was after that session that she started to unwind, physically and emotionally. Each week she softened more and she talked more. Eventually, she came off her antidepressants and stopped coming for reflexology.

Then one day, she came back into my clinic, half laughing, half fuming. "I could kill you, Ruth!" she said. I had no idea what I'd done. "My feet have gone up a whole shoe size," she grinned. "I've had to buy all new shoes. It's cost me a fortune!"

We both laughed and I still smile when I think of it. Once she had let go of all the tension, anger, and pain she'd been holding, her feet had literally softened and expanded. Just like her energy.

Our bodies reflect what we carry, even when we think we've buried it well.

Because I believe so deeply in the connection between body, mind, and soul, I've structured this book into three parts. In each part, we'll explore simple, practical ways to nourish yourself.

We'll begin with the body, looking at the physical causes of deep fatigue and how changes in diet and lifestyle can help you rebuild your health. From there, we'll move to the mind, exploring ways to ease stress and support resilience in your daily life. Finally, we'll turn to the soul, opening up space to release emotional burdens and free up energy.

At the end of the book, you'll also find a section on herbs and homeopathic remedies that may support you on your journey.

IS THERE A PART OF YOU THAT'S SCARED OF CHANGE?

One of my patients, a psychologist, once wrote to me and said:

"Everything we do works for us in some way or another. Even if we think we aren't getting anything out of it. It's called secondary gain. My chronic fatigue is the thing that has kept me safe. It's the excuse I use not to put myself out there. And if I don't try, I don't fail - right?"

This is such an important insight. Psychologists use the term *secondary gain* to describe the hidden benefits we get from symptoms, even when those symptoms make us miserable. And neuroscience backs this up: our brains are wired to choose safety over growth. If your exhaustion protects you from risk, failure, or painful emotions, your nervous system may unconsciously hold onto it - not because you want to be tired, but because a part of you feels safer that way.

Think about it: change always carries uncertainty, and our brains are wired to prefer the familiar over the unknown. As the old saying goes, *"better the devil you know."* So even if part of you longs for more energy, another part may cling to fatigue because, in its own way, it feels safer. It's a form of protection.

I know this personally. There was a long stretch of my life where I kept myself so busy, and so utterly exhausted, that I had no time or energy to look at the hard things I had gone through in my childhood.

12

My burnout was a great excuse not to think, not to probe, not to explore who I really was. It was an excuse to ignore myself. It was my protection.

Unfortunately, although it kept me safe from the pain of exploring who I was and where I came from, it also prevented me growing or moving forward.

So I'd like you to pause here and reflect. Grab your journal and ask yourself:

- o How am I benefiting from being this tired?
- o What is my exhaustion protecting me from?
- o What might I have to face if I had more energy?
- o Who would I challenge or disappoint if I suddenly had the strength to change?
- o What do I fear might happen if I were well?

These are not easy questions. But even if you can answer just one of them honestly, you'll begin to uncover what your body's been trying to tell you all along. And remember - none of this means you are "choosing" to be unwell. It means your body and mind are doing their best to keep you safe. Your task now is to gently reassure yourself that you are ready for more than survival. You are ready to grow.

YOUR STORY MATTERS

"Owning our story can be hard but not nearly as difficult as spending our lives running from it."
- Brene Brown

I once went through all my patients' notes to see if I could find a pattern in the causes of fatigue. I was stunned at what I found.

Every single one of my patients with deep fatigue had experienced trauma, grief, or loss of personal power at some stage in their life.

13

Causes included loss of a loved one, nursing of a sick parent or sibling, living in a home with alcoholism or addiction, experiencing repeated abuse be it verbal, physical or sexual, losing one's home or immigrating to a new country.

However, what I found most interesting when reading through my notes was that despite such painful experiences, all these individuals had intentionally chosen to move away from their pain and had spoken about their past in terms of having 'dealt' with it already. Put it all behind them.

When they came to see me, they felt they were strong. Yet they were all tired. They had an emptiness inside them.

I know that emptiness well. I know what it's like to need to be strong, to keep moving, to get on with things. To not let the past hold you back.

It wasn't until I was in my 40s that I could talk about my dad with any sense of ease - without feeling pain or shame. He took his own life when I was six, and for some reason, I grew up thinking I wasn't good enough for him to want to stay alive. We never spoke about him at home, and I never spoke about him to my friends. I was too ashamed.

To be honest, there was a time I used to lie about it. If someone new asked how he died, I'd say he was shot in the Rhodesian war. Yet he wasn't.

Funny how there are parts of ourselves we just can't accept.

But it's that *not accepting* that makes us so tired. It's the constant running from ourselves.

It's taken me years to feel at peace with what happened in our home when I was six. I still feel sad when I think about him. It still hurts. But the empty void isn't there anymore.

What about you? What is your story? If you feel tired, empty and as if there is a void somewhere deep inside of you, then I'd like to gently invite you to take some time to look at where you've come from and how you've arrived at where you now are.

WRITE YOUR STORY

Slow down and write your story. Take a pen and paper, set aside some quiet time, and begin with your earliest memories. Where did you come from? Who were your parents? What were they like?

Don't be afraid to write down the parts that have hurt you, as well as the parts that have helped you. You can only release and reshape your story once you've acknowledged the one you've lived.

When you read it back, you might be surprised by your own strength. When you see your life mapped out in front of you, you'll see how much you've been through. Take a moment to acknowledge your journey and the strength it has taken for you to get to where you now are in life. Take a moment to say *well done* to yourself. To say *thank you* to yourself.

I recently heard Tunde Oyeneyin share her story of loss and grief. Within six years, she lost both her parents and her brother. With each loss, she described herself sinking lower and lower. Her story was heartbreaking to hear until she said:

"We don't get to choose what happens to us, but we do get to choose how we react… I am who I am in my mind, in my body, in my spirit, in all that I do because of what I've learned in my lowest moment."

Her words are a reminder that while we cannot rewrite the past, we can choose how we carry it forward. By acknowledging our story, we create the space to shape what comes next.

2, BEGIN WHERE YOU ARE

"Illness is not an interruption of life, but a crucial and valuable effort to reach for more wholeness of spirit."
- Rudolph Ballentine

I love doing jigsaw puzzles and there are a few things you learn when you're working on one. For example, the puzzle isn't complete if you leave out the pieces you don't like; it takes time and patience to complete a puzzle; and, the more you try to rush the puzzle, the more frustrating it becomes. It also helps to start the puzzle with something solid, like the outside edges, before moving into the more complicated centre.

Recovering from deep fatigue is much the same. We can't ignore or leave out parts of ourselves that we don't like; healing takes time and a lot of patience; and the more we try to rush rebuilding our health, the more frustrated we become. It really is a lesson in slowing down!

Similar to starting a puzzle with the outside edges, it helps to begin the healing journey with a solid baseline - something we can see and measure our progress against. At the end of this chapter, you'll find a simple 'Health Check-In' form that I encourage you to take a few minutes to complete. Doing so will help you reflect on where you are right now and give you a baseline from which you can track changes as they occur.

16

Tracking measurable changes will help motivate you. Just like with a massive jigsaw puzzle, you might find yourself feeling overwhelmed by how much there is to do and you might feel like you're pushing a boulder uphill, only for it to roll right back down again. Tracking your improvements, even the tiniest ones, will help remind you that things are shifting. When there's so much going on, it's easy to miss the little pieces that are quietly falling into place. And if you don't notice those changes, it's easy to feel deflated - even when you're making progress.

I strongly recommend you visit your doctor before starting anything suggested in this book. There are two reasons for this. Firstly I, as a writer, do not know what is going on with your health right now. Your doctor will be able to advise you if any of my suggestions are not suitable for your current health condition. Secondly, your doctor can run some tests to give you a clearer picture of your current health status and help you establish a baseline. They can also help you identify, or rule out, any underlying health conditions that may be contributing to your fatigue, such as anaemia or hypothyroidism.

HEALTH CONDITIONS ASSOCIATED WITH FATIGUE

Before we go any further we'll take a look at two conditions that are commonly associated with fatigue – anaemia and hypothyroidism. You may already have been diagnosed with one of them. I like to refer to them as 'chicken-and-egg' conditions because they cause fatigue, but at the same time people with burnout or chronic fatigue tend to develop them and it's often difficult to know which came first.

I'll give you a brief introduction to each condition as well as some tips on how to help manage them at home. Please note – and this is really important – this book is not a replacement for medical care. Everything I suggest here should be used in combination with what your doctor recommends.

ANAEMIA (LOW IRON LEVELS)

Anaemia can cause fatigue, low immunity, headaches, and dizziness. If you're constantly tired and also have symptoms like frequent infections, slow-healing skin, easy bruising, dizziness, pale skin, or are always feeling cold, I suggest asking your doctor to check your iron levels.

What to Ask Your Doctor

Ask for an iron studies blood test. The most important result to look at is your ferritin level, which shows how much iron your body is storing. Even if your other results are normal, low ferritin means your iron stores are depleted.

Your doctor may recommend iron supplements. These should be taken away from tannin-rich drinks like tea and calcium-rich foods like milk, yoghurt or breakfast cereals, as these can block absorption. Taking them with vitamin C, for example an orange, will help absorption.

Iron supplements can sometimes cause digestive discomfort or constipation. If that happens, try taking them at night before bed, at least two hours after eating. Or ask your doctor about switching to a gentler form of iron.

Natural Support: Food and Herbs

Diet and herbs can help increase your iron levels. Red meat, egg yolks, leafy greens and raisins are all rich in iron. Eating a variety of these foods regularly can make a big difference.

Nettles (*Urtica dioica*), alfalfa (*Medicago sativa*), and dandelion leaf (*Taraxacum officinale*) are herbs rich in iron and minerals. You can grow nettles and dandelions in your garden (they're technically weeds, but I think they're nutrient bombs) or buy them as teas or tinctures from a health food store or your herbalist. These herbs are deeply nourishing and supportive for rebuilding energy.

Blackstrap molasses is another natural option I recommend to many of my patients. Just make sure it's organic! Add a tablespoon to a mug of hot water and sip it like tea. The taste isn't great, but you get used to it.

Look for the Root Cause

Our bodies are designed to function well so when something's off, there's always a reason. If you're anaemic, it's important to understand *why*.

Some common causes include:

- o Poor diet
- o Heavy periods
- o Blood loss (e.g., from childbirth or injury)
- o Poor iron absorption due to gut issues (we'll explore this in Chapter 7)
- o Gastrointestinal bleeding (e.g., ulcers or haemorrhoids)
- o Low B12 or folate
- o Growth spurts in children or teens
- o Intense athletic training or over-exercise.

Certain infections, both bacterial and viral, can also interfere with iron absorption or red blood cell production. If you're still feeling tired despite taking iron, ask your doctor about testing for hidden infections. We'll look at some of these infections later in this chapter.

HYPOTHYROIDISM (UNDERACTIVE THYROID)

If, in addition to always feeling tired, you've gained a lot of weight, your skin and hair have become dry, your hair is falling out or thinning, you're struggling with constipation, feeling depressed, have irregular periods and are experiencing brain fog then you may have an underactive thyroid (hypothyroidism). Your thyroid gland controls your metabolism - the process by which your body transforms the food you eat into energy. The thyroid affects every aspect of your health and, if you're a woman, it also plays a big role in hormonal balance.

What to Ask Your Doctor

Getting your thyroid function properly tested can be difficult. Many people experience all the symptoms of an underactive thyroid, but their blood tests fall within the "normal" range, and they don't receive a diagnosis. In some countries, the standard test only checks for TSH (thyroid-stimulating hormone), which doesn't give the full picture.

I suggest you write down all your symptoms and take that list to your doctor. Ask for a full thyroid function test that includes:

o **TSH (thyroid-stimulating hormone):** Made by your pituitary gland, TSH acts like a "messenger," telling your thyroid how much hormone to make. If the level of thyroid hormones in your blood is too low, your pituitary releases more TSH to encourage your thyroid to produce more. If the levels are too high, it releases less TSH.

o **Free T4 (thyroxine):** This is the main hormone your thyroid releases. It's mostly inactive at this stage and needs to be converted into T3 before your body can use it.

o **Free T3 (triiodothyronine):** This is the active form of thyroid hormone – the one your cells actually use to make energy and keep your metabolism running smoothly.

o **Thyroid antibodies:** Your TSH, T3, and T4 levels can be perfectly normal even if your antibodies are elevated. This means your immune system may be quietly attacking your thyroid in the background. This can cause symptoms even when your test results look fine on paper.

Your body naturally converts T4 into T3, but this process can slow down if you're stressed, dealing with inflammation, or not getting enough of certain nutrients. Later in this book, we'll look at gentle, natural ways to support this process and help your thyroid work at its best.

If hypothyroidism is diagnosed, your doctor will prescribe you medication such as thyroxine. Many people feel better once their hormone levels are stabilised. And while there's currently no medical treatment for thyroid antibodies, there's a lot you can do with natural support. If your antibody levels are high, I recommend seeing a qualified herbalist or homoeopath who can help support your thyroid gently and holistically. Thyroid health is integral to every aspect of your physical, mental and even emotional health. So please don't waste time or money trying to fix it with home remedies. See a professional!

Natural Support: Food and Herbs

Your thyroid plays such an important role in the health of your whole body, so if it's underactive, it's important to follow your doctor's advice and treat it properly. The information below is here to support you but it's not a substitute for medical care.

Eating a variety of mineral-rich whole foods will support your thyroid, especially foods high in iodine (seaweed, fish), selenium (Brazil nuts, sunflower seeds), zinc (pumpkin seeds, shellfish, eggs) and iron (see anaemia section).

One of the best herbs for thyroid support is Ashwagandha (*Withania somnifera*). It's an adaptogen which means it helps balance the stress response – if you're feeling flat, it can help restore energy; if you're stressed or overstimulated, it can help calm the system. It also nourishes the adrenal glands, helps you sleep and supports immunity. It's generally safe in small amounts for an underactive thyroid, but check with a qualified herbalist if you're on medication or have an overactive thyroid.

Look for the Root Cause

If your thyroid is underactive, it's important to ask why. If your blood tests show thyroid antibodies, it means your immune system is mistakenly targeting your thyroid. We call this an autoimmune condition. Possible contributors to autoimmunity are long-term stress, chronic inflammation, poor gut health (including poor nutrition, malabsorption, and food-intolerances), and hormonal changes. We will look at all of these in more depth later in the book.

OTHER CAUSES OF CONSTANT TIREDNESS

In addition to anaemia and hypothyroidism, there are other common causes of fatigue that you should rule out. I'll briefly introduce them here.

Infections

When you start exploring infections linked to chronic fatigue it can feel like opening a can of worms because there are just so many possible culprits. So, I want to gently offer a word of caution here: trying to pinpoint one specific infection as the cause of your fatigue can become a long, expensive, and often frustrating journey. In some cases, working with an integrative doctor to explore possible infections may be helpful but I encourage you not to lose yourself in the search because even when something is identified, there may be no clear medical treatment available. Instead of spending all your time and energy chasing one root cause, focus on rebuilding and strengthening your body as a whole. That's what the protocol in this book is here to support you with.

Having said that, there are a few well-known infections associated with chronic fatigue, including Lyme disease (*Borrelia burgdorferi* and *Borrelia mayonii*), Epstein-Barr virus (EBV) and cytomegalovirus (CMV). Your doctor can do blood or stool tests for these and although there is currently no known medical treatment for them, there are both homoeopathic and herbal solutions.

Low-grade lung, gut and dental infections can also contribute to an ongoing inflammatory response that leads to fatigue. We'll explore chronic inflammation in Chapter 5.

Nutrient Deficiencies

The B-vitamins are essential for keeping your nervous system healthy, producing energy, and supporting a balanced mood. I often call them the "stress vitamins" because your body uses them up quickly during times of pressure, illness, or emotional strain. Low levels can leave you with:

- o Ongoing fatigue or low energy
- o Brain fog, poor concentration, forgetfulness
- o Low mood, irritability or feeling "flat"
- o Tingling, numbness or burning sensations in hands or feet
- o Cracks at the corners of your mouth
- o A sore, red tongue
- o A sense of weakness or aching muscles
- o Shortness of breath or palpitations (from anaemia)
- o Hair loss or skin rashes.

If you notice several of these symptoms, speak to your doctor and ask for a blood test to check your vitamin B levels. If they are low, then focus on eating B-vitamin-rich foods such as:

- o Liver (beef, chicken, or lamb) – liver is one of the richest sources of nearly all your B-vitamins
- o Eggs – especially the yolks
- o Meat – beef, pork, lamb, chicken, and turkey
- o Fish and seafood – salmon, tuna, trout, mackerel, sardines, shellfish
- o Dairy products – milk, yoghurt, cheese
- o Whole grains – oats, brown rice, barley, rye

- o Legumes – lentils, chickpeas, black beans, kidney beans
- o Leafy greens – spinach, kale, silverbeet, romaine lettuce
- o Seeds and nuts – sunflower seeds, almonds, walnuts
- o Avocado – especially good for B5 (pantothenic acid).

Eating a variety of these foods each day will help you cover the full spectrum of B-vitamins and keep your energy systems supported.

The other nutrient that plays a central role in maintaining your energy levels is vitamin D. But, believe it or not, vitamin D is not a vitamin at all - it's what's known as a prohormone. While it's not usually thought of as an "energy nutrient," low vitamin D can affect how your body absorbs minerals, weaken your immune function, and lead to muscle aches, bone pain, low mood, and fatigue.

Your doctor can run a simple blood test to assess your vitamin D levels. They may be low if you rarely spend time outdoors, work night shifts, or live in a polluted or low-sunlight area.

The easiest way to boost your vitamin D is to spend time in natural sunlight. Just 10 to 20 minutes on your skin each day (without sunscreen) can make a difference. Food sources include oily fish (like salmon and sardines), egg yolks, mushrooms, and fortified foods like plant-based milks or cereals.

Medications

Fatigue is a common side effect of many prescription medications. This includes drugs used to treat high blood pressure, high cholesterol, reflux, allergies, depression, anxiety, and insomnia. If you've started feeling more tired since beginning a new medication, it's worth looking into.

Please don't stop taking any medication on your own but do speak with your doctor. They may be able to adjust your dosage or recommend an alternative medication that works better for your energy levels.

Chronic Inflammation, Gut Imbalances, or Food Intolerances

Ongoing fatigue can often be linked to underlying inflammation, gut imbalances like leaky gut or dysbiosis, and sensitivities to certain foods. These issues can also show up as joint pain, skin rashes, allergies, headaches, or brain fog. We'll explore all of these in more depth later in the book including how to support and gently rebuild your gut.

Menstrual Issues and Menopause

Many women experience heavy, painful, or frequent periods which can be exhausting and even debilitating over time. And unfortunately, the more depleted you become, the more irregular and difficult your cycle can get. Good nutrition, rest, and a balanced routine can help regulate your hormones and support your energy. We'll explore this more throughout the book.

Fatigue is also very common during menopause, especially when sleep is disrupted by hot flushes or night sweats. Women who are already burnt out or exhausted often find menopause symptoms harder to manage.

If you're struggling with both hormones and fatigue, start by visiting your doctor to check for anaemia or hypothyroidism, as both are closely linked to fatigue in women. Once these are addressed, see a homoeopath or herbalist for your menstrual or menopausal symptoms. You won't be able to restore your energy until your hormones are balanced, so make this a priority.

ARE YOU READY TO START?

We don't wake up one day and, out of nowhere, feel burned out. It creeps in slowly, day by day. Often, we ignore it and push through until we've been so tired for so long that it feels like it's the only way to be. We forget what it's like to feel different, and because exhaustion has been our constant companion, we start to believe it's normal. As Michael Gervais says, "We become the stories that we tell ourselves."

Worse still, we convince ourselves that this is how we'll feel for the rest of our lives. So, let's break that cycle right now with a quick exercise.

Take out your journal and turn to a blank page. Grab a stopwatch and set it for two minutes. For two minutes you'll write as quickly as you can without stopping to think or edit. This is important - you don't want to overthink things.

Picture yourself five years from today: you're completely healthy, brimming with energy, and feeling incredible. You're fit, vibrant, and living the life you've always dreamed of.

For the next two minutes, write down what you see in this vision. Use the present tense only. For example, I'm walking along the beach or I'm playing with my kids. Describe where you are, what you're doing, what you're wearing, and who you're with.

There are no limits to this vision. It's five years from now and you have all the time, energy, and health you could imagine. Let yourself enjoy the process, have fun with it, and allow yourself to dream.

Once the timer is up, read what you wrote and choose just one thing that stands out and truly resonates with you. Now ask yourself: What kind of person does that?

I did this exercise with my client Maxine. She had been told she needed to lose weight before knee surgery. She came to me tired and frustrated after repeatedly failing at diets.

We did this exercise and her vision of health was playing basketball with her sons - something her weight prevented. When I asked how she could achieve it, she said, "Stop eating so much and lose 35kg." An overwhelming goal!

I encouraged her to reframe things, focusing on the kind of person who plays basketball with her sons. She said: "I'm the kind of person who chooses foods that build and strengthen my body." So much more inspiring!

The aim of this exercise is to help you realise that how you're feeling right now is not how you will feel for the rest of your life. This exhausted, empty vessel you think is "you" isn't the real you. It's just a phase, a moment in time. You're stuck in a pocket of life, but you have a beautiful, inspiring future ahead.

This exercise is not about goals or resolutions but about reconnecting with a part of you that still believes in possibility.

YOUR HEALTH CHECK-IN: A PERSONAL BASELINE

To track your improvements, it helps to take note of exactly where you are now. Here is a 'Health Check-In' to help you get a clear baseline from which you can move forward.

I suggest you complete this check-in today before you start making any of the changes given in this book. Please don't let it overwhelm you or stir up feelings of shame or guilt. Try to see it as simply witnessing where you are so that over time, you can track how you're moving forward.

Repeat this check-in every three months as you follow the guidelines in this book. It's also a good idea to take some clear, honest photos of what you look like now. You'll be amazed at how different you'll look in a few years' time.

Yes, I did say a few years. As happened with my reflexology client, it took over a year before her feet changed size.

Healing happens slowly.

My Health Check-In

*Date:*_____

Height	
Weight	
Waist	
Hips	

How to take your measurements:
- Waist: Use a tape measure to measure the circumference of your waist using your belly button as a reference. Measure three times and take the average.
- Hips: Measure your hips at their widest part. Measure three times and take the average.

Record Your Current Health Status

Blood pressure	
Pulse rate	
Allergies	
Intolerances	
Medication	
Supplements, herbs, remedies	

Describe your current health in as much detail as possible:

Record Your Current Symptoms

Go through the following list and circle any symptoms you've been experiencing. Next to each one, note how many days a week it shows up, and rate its severity out of 10 (e.g. mild headache = 2/10, migraine that puts you in bed = 9/10). Over time, you may still have these symptoms but hopefully less often and less intensely.

Sore throat	
Frequent infections	
Muscle or joint pain	
Headaches or migraines	
Brain fog	
Poor memory	
Difficulty concentrating	

Dizziness/light-headedness	
Heart palpitations (noticeable heartbeat)	
Cravings for caffeine, sugar or alcohol	
Food cravings	
Food intolerances	
Skin rashes	
Hay fever, sinus issues, postnasal drip	
Fatigue after exercise	
Insomnia	
Nightmares or bad dreams	
Night sweats	
Premenstrual tension (PMS)	
Period problems	
Fatigue or illness around ovulation	
Other	

PART 1. NOURISH YOUR BODY

3, Eat To Create Energy

"There will come a time when you believe everything is finished; that will be the beginning."
- Louis L'Amour

How strange that I'm beginning this chapter by quoting an American novelist who wrote about cowboys! The truth is, I love his words. If you feel as if everything is finished, if you want to give up and stop trying, then you're in the right place. You're exactly where you need to be right now.

You're at that point where you have no choice but to start again and the best place to start is by creating energy one meal at a time. The easiest way to do this is to set up a routine – a simple action plan you can follow without having to think too much.

Although we often think that our thoughts create our reality, when it comes to fatigue and burnout with all its brain fog and poor concentration, I tend to agree with world-renowned neurologist David Perlmutter who says: "our actions create our thoughts". Think about it – if you're struggling with brain fog, poor concentration or memory problems, if your head feels like its filled with cotton wool, then what kind of reality does that create?

So let's start with a simple action plan that will help you develop some energy and mental clarity - easy habits that don't require much thinking but gently steady your system.

The next few chapters focus heavily on eating habits. They may feel familiar or even repetitive, but I linger on these basics because, done consistently, they work. Take a few weeks to move slowly through them and practise these basics until they become habits. As your body steadies, your mental energy will follow and when you feel clearer, you can move onto Parts 2 and 3, where the deep healing really begins.

As we cover the basics, I'll share lists of nourishing foods and simple habits. For easy reference, every list is gathered at the back of the book in A Simple Food Guide.

START WITH WHERE YOU ARE

Before we go further, get a clear picture of your current eating habits. Grab your journal, write today's date at the top of a page and record everything you've eaten and drunk today, yesterday and the day before. This will help you see your habits and any patterns of which you may not be aware.

Then on a new sheet of paper make two lists: one of your favourite meals, foods and drinks and the other of foods and drinks that you really dislike.

These lists will form the basis of your meal plans and as you move through this chapter, choose only from the foods you enjoy and adapt them to be healthier. There's no need to force down things you don't like just because they're "healthy."

Now let's get an idea of how your current eating habits are affecting your everyday life. Get your journal again and write down your answers to the following questions. It's important to record how you are feeling now so that you can go back to this in a few months and hopefully notice some changes.

Do you currently:

- O Struggle with brain fog?
- O Often feel light-headed?
- O Get irritable or short-tempered when you haven't eaten for a while?
- O Crave chocolate, chips, bread, pasta, or sugary/starchy foods?
- O Find it hard to lose weight, no matter how strict your diet or how much you exercise?
- O Get recurrent infections, especially fungal ones like thrush?

BALANCE YOUR BLOOD SUGAR, BOOST YOUR ENERGY

If you answered yes to the questions above, you may have a condition called hypoglycaemia. It's often referred to as low blood sugar levels or low blood glucose levels. Sugar, or glucose, is the energy source for every cell in your body. When your cells need to work, to function, to reproduce, to do anything – they need energy, and they get that energy from glucose.

So where does glucose come from? It comes from the food you eat. Whatever you eat is broken down into glucose and carried around your body in your blood.

At any given moment, your body only needs about one teaspoon of sugar circulating in your blood. Too much can lead to high blood glucose levels (hyperglycaemia), and too little can lead to low blood glucose levels (hypoglycaemia). Both of these can become dangerous if left untreated so it's important to have balanced blood sugars. Not too high and not too low.

Low blood glucose levels are common in people with fatigue and can be diagnosed through blood tests.

Symptoms include:

- o Fatigue
- o Mood swings (irritability and/or tearfulness)
- o Poor concentration
- o Trembling, shaking, weakness
- o Hunger and/or food cravings
- o Light headedness and dizziness.

When you have low blood glucose levels you'll instinctively reach for a sugar-fix such as a coke, muffin or large bowl of pasta to help bring your blood sugars up. These cravings are normal and your body's instinctive way of trying to get energy as quickly as possible.

Refined carbohydrates like bread, pasta, biscuits, cakes, chocolate and sweets (oh, the list is endless!) break down quickly into glucose. That might sound helpful, especially when you're tired, because they give you an energy boost. But here's the catch: that sudden glucose spike can be seen as dangerous by your body. So, your body releases hormones to bring your blood sugar down. If levels drop too low and there's no steady supply of glucose, your cells start to panic. They send signals to your brain: We need fuel!

As a result, you get hungry. But not just hungry - you instinctively crave foods you know will break down rapidly into glucose. For example, sugar. This is why you get energy crashes followed by cravings for quick sources of glucose such as sugar and refined carbohydrates. It's like being on a roller-coaster of energy crashes and sugar cravings.

If you're on that blood sugar roller-coaster for too long, you can develop what's known as insulin resistance. Insulin is the hormone that helps glucose move from your bloodstream into your cells. Think of insulin as a little key that opens a door, allowing glucose inside to be used for energy.

When there's too much glucose in your blood too often, your body releases more and more insulin. Over time, your cells become less responsive to it. It's as if they're saying, "We've had enough of you. We're changing the locks!"

As insulin resistance develops, your cells struggle to take in glucose, and your energy levels drop. To compensate, your body produces even more insulin, creating a vicious cycle.

Your doctor can test for insulin resistance by checking both fasting glucose and fasting insulin levels. Common signs include fatigue, brain fog, weight gain (especially around the belly), sugar cravings, and energy crashes.

If left unaddressed, insulin resistance can increase your risk of type 2 diabetes, heart disease, non-alcoholic fatty liver disease (NAFLD), and for women, polycystic ovary syndrome (PCOS).

Hopefully by now you can see how important it is to control your blood glucose levels.

THE SECRET TO BALANCING YOUR BLOOD SUGARS

So how do you step off that roller-coaster of cravings and crashes?

First of all, don't try to starve yourself or restrict your diet too heavily - doing so will only leave you feeling worse and craving sugar even more. Instead, start by eating in a way that balances your blood sugar.

And how do you do that? It's surprisingly simple as there are only three rules you need to follow:

1. Eat healthy proteins and good fats with every meal
2. Eat plenty of vegetables
3. Move your body every day.

EAT HEALTHY PROTEINS AND GOOD FATS WITH EVERY MEAL

Proteins and fats are complex molecules which break down slowly and are longer-lasting sources of energy than carbohydrates. When you include them with your meals, your blood glucose levels stay stable and you're less likely to need a snack an hour or two later. These foods help reduce cravings, ease mood swings, and prevent energy crashes.

So what do I mean by healthy proteins and good fats? Here are some examples.

Animal sources:
- o Meat
- o Eggs
- o Fish, especially oily fish such as sardines, mackerel, and salmon
- o Full-cream dairy

Plant sources:
- o Nuts and seeds
- o Soy-based products such as tempeh, tofu and edamame
- o Legumes such as lentils, chickpeas, beans and split peas
- o Sprouted legumes
- o Quinoa, amaranth, buckwheat
- o Avocados
- o Olives
- o Cold-pressed oils like olive, coconut, macadamia, and avocado
- o Nutritional yeast.

When rebuilding your health, you need to ensure you provide your body with the best possible building blocks and that you minimize toxins, preservatives, colourants and hormones in your diet. Always choose simple, natural sources of protein such as grass-fed meats or free-range dairy and avoid trans fats or partially hydrogenated fats such as those used in deep-frying and fast-food venues.

Earlier in this chapter I asked you to write down everything you've eaten or drunk over the last few days. Have a look at that list now and see if you can connect your energy crashes to your eating habits.

If you regularly get a mid-morning crash, look at your breakfast. Do you even eat breakfast? If you crave a coffee and muffin late afternoon, could it be because lunch was just a light salad or sandwich? Think of children – when they're hungry they get irritable and moody. So do we!

Here are some easy ways to ensure you eat to balance your blood sugars:

- o Having a sandwich for lunch? Make sure it includes some protein like meat, fish, cheese, or egg. Skip the plain jam sandwich.
- o Craving chocolate or a biscuit this afternoon? That's okay, enjoy it! Just pair it with a handful of nuts or a slice of cheese to slow the sugar hit.
- o Want a coke or a glass of wine? Go ahead but have it with a proper meal, not on its own.

Do you get the picture? We often mistakenly think we need to give up everything we love to be healthy. But we actually don't! We need to understand how the body works and work with it, not against it.

But What About Sugar?

You may be wondering whether you need to give up refined sugar completely. In an ideal world, the answer is yes. But in reality, cutting out all refined sugar at once can feel overwhelming and add even more stress to an already busy life.

A gentler approach is to first focus on balancing your blood sugars by adding healthy fats and proteins to your meals. Once that foundation is in place, it becomes much easier to reduce, and eventually cut out, refined sugar and artificial sweeteners.

If you love sweet things, try having raw, unheated honey or pure maple syrup instead of refined white sugar. Both contain trace minerals and tend to raise blood sugar more gently than processed sugar.

Also, as much as possible, avoid artificial sweeteners. They may seem like a healthier swap, but many disrupt your microbiome, increase cravings for sugar, and confuse your body's ability to regulate blood sugar. Rather opt for honey or maple syrup.

EAT PLENTY OF VEGETABLES

Vegetables, especially your leafy greens and colourful vegetables, are rich in fibre. Fibre slows down the release of glucose into your bloodstream, which helps to keep your blood sugar more stable.

Vegetables also nourish your gut and reduce inflammation - two important factors in reversing insulin resistance and topics we will dive into more deeply later in the book.

MOVE YOUR BODY EVERY DAY

Movement helps your muscles use up glucose from your bloodstream and improves how your body responds to insulin. Daily movement is one of the easiest and most effective ways to support blood sugar balance.

However, if you're living with fatigue, you may find that exercise leaves you feeling worse - more tired, achy, or foggy. This is known as post-exertional malaise, and it occurs when exercise (or stress) triggers a flare-up of symptoms.

That's why I've suggested you move every day, rather than exercise every day. Gentle walks, stretching, or light activity is often enough.

Start small, listen to your body, and build up gradually as your energy improves.

YOUR FIRST HABIT SHIFT

Remember David Perlmutter's words, "your actions create your thoughts"? Let's work with that idea by beginning a few small daily actions that, over time, will help clear your foggy brain. Once you're thinking more clearly, you'll have more energy to take on the deeper work I'll invite you into later in this book.

For the next two to three weeks, we'll focus on eating for energy. I'll guide you step by step through a few simple habit shifts designed to help stabilise your blood sugar. When your blood sugar is balanced, your energy will improve and so will your mental clarity.

Let's begin.

STEP 1: PREPARE

- **Write a list** of your favourite vegetables, healthy proteins and good fats.
- **Stick it on your fridge** as a daily reminder to include them with every meal and snack.
- **Take a photo** of the list and save it on your phone to remind you what to buy when you go shopping.
- **Now go shopping.** If you're too tired today, do an online shop or ask a friend to stop by the shops for you. It's vital that you have some good food in your house as soon as possible.
- **Have some pre-prepared snacks** in your fridge or pantry for those days when you're too tired to cook. For example:
- Boiled eggs (keep the shells on until needed)
- A shop-cooked rotisserie chicken

o   Tins of fish or legumes - mackerel, tuna, sardines, beans, lentils or chickpeas
o   Avocadoes when they're in season
o   Nuts and seeds (I keep some in my handbag and car for emergency snacks)
o   Sprouts and seaweed
o   Protein-rich soups such as chicken, beef, or miso
o   Tofu or tempeh.

Preparation really is key when it comes to rebuilding your health. So is doing what's easy. Don't make being healthy complicated or time-consuming.

STEP 2: EAT A GOOD PROTEIN OR GOOD FAT WITH EVERY MEAL AND EVERY SNACK

From today onwards, focus on eating a healthy protein or good fat, or both, with every meal and snack - especially when you're having something sweet like alcohol or sugary foods. For now, don't worry about your weight or 'eating healthily'. Only focus on balancing your blood sugars.

When your blood sugars are stabilised everything else will become easier. You'll have more energy, better moods, and fewer cravings. Then you will find it easier to overhaul your diet if you wish to.

I want to emphasise here that this is not a "low-carb" or "keto" diet. This is not even a diet! All you're doing is carrying on with how you normally eat and simply adding in a healthy protein or healthy fat every time you have a meal or a snack.

Don't try to give up anything you love just yet. If you usually have biscuits with your afternoon tea, keep eating them and enjoy them. Simply add in the good stuff – have a handful of almond nuts with your biscuits, or half an avocado before your biscuits.

It usually takes about two to three weeks for blood sugars to stabilise. You'll know they're stable when your energy feels steadier, your sugar-cravings ease, and you're not getting that shaky hunger between meals.

STEP 3: ADD 2 CUPS OF VEGETABLES TO YOUR MEALS

Leafy greens and brightly coloured vegetables are rich in fibre, which helps slow the release of glucose into your bloodstream and supports more balanced energy. Try to include at least two cups of vegetables with every meal. Cook them in different ways and mix up the colours and types so you don't get bored.

I also want to gently highlight that while vegetables are your focus here, it's best not to increase your fruit intake at the same time. Although fruit is full of vitamins and naturally nutritious, it's also high in natural sugars and can raise blood glucose more quickly, especially when eaten on its own. Until your blood sugar levels are more stable, try limiting fruit to one or two servings a day, and always pair it with a healthy fat or protein to help keep your energy steady.

SET YOURSELF UP FOR SUCCESS

"If you want to play the game and win, you've got to make the game winnable."
– Tony Robbins

Changing eating habits is hard, especially when your energy is low so here are some tips to help you set yourself up for success:

- o **Be honest with yourself.** This is your health journey and the more personal and honest you make it, the more you'll enjoy it.
- o **Be kind to yourself.** As you work through this book, you'll realise that I see perfection as the enemy. You don't have to do everything I suggest perfectly. You will have

good days and you will have bad days. And that's okay. Just keep going.

o **Make only one change at a time. Don't be in a rush.** As Mae West said, "All things worth doing are worth doing slowly." It will take time for you to rebuild your health and if you keep expecting to see big changes quickly you will end up frustrated and depressed. Just take one small step at a time and one day you'll look back and be amazed at how far you've come.

o **Create habits that are easy, enjoyable and that fit in with who you are,** what you want from life and how you want to live your life. If you do this, you'll create habits you can stick to.

o **Focus on energy and abundance, not restrictions or limitations.** Time and again I've seen people not only fail but also exhaust themselves with a new health regime because they give up everything they love in life. Remember, you're not doing a "diet" here, you're creating new habits that will hopefully last a lifetime. Don't choose to eat lentils for the rest of your life if you don't like them!

Think about energy - it's not stagnant, it flows. To create more energy in your life, try not to restrict or limit yourself. Restrictive diets and rigid routines don't support flow. Energy comes from a feeling of abundance, not restraint.

And remember…

Create healthy habits that can carry you when you're too tired to think.

o Stock your fridge and pantry with your favourite healthy proteins and good fats

o Keep some healthy pre-cooked or ready-to-eat proteins or fats on hand for days when cooking feels too hard

o Eat a good protein or fat with every meal and snack

45

- o Eat two cupful's of vegetables with every meal
- o Move your body every day.

Go gently. This is about creating energy, not perfection.

4, EAT TO BUILD YOUR BODY

Here's a small exercise for you. Look at your hands, your nails, your skin. Visualise what's beneath your skin: your muscles, bones, veins and arteries. Can you picture your heart? Can you feel it beating? What about your lungs? Take a moment to feel them expand as you inhale.

Now go deeper. Down into the tiny cells that make up your lungs, heart, arteries, veins, bones, muscles, skin and nails. Picture those cells. See the nucleus in charge. The mitochondria working hard to create energy. The specialised structures detoxing and cleaning.

Now ask yourself: what are those cellular structures made of? What are your cells made of? Where do they come from?

The answer is simple.

They're built from elements like carbon, oxygen, hydrogen, nitrogen, sodium, and potassium. And all these elements are supplied by the food you eat.

You are literally what you eat. Put junk in, and you'll get junk out. Put in nourishing, nutritious food, and you'll build a strong, healthy body.

The average person eats around 500 kg of food a year. When you think about it, how much of that is truly nourishing? What percentage of that builds a healthy body, and how much is junk? Sometimes when I'm deciding what to eat, I think of these words by Ann Wigmore: "The food you eat can be either the safest and most powerful form of medicine or the slowest form of poison."

When you're at the start of a health journey, it can be easy to get depressed and give up but there is something important that I want you to keep in mind as you're rebuilding your health: the body you have today is not the body you'll have in a few years' time. Damaged or diseased cells are constantly being replaced and your body really can heal itself if you give it the right building blocks.

Whatever you choose to do today will affect your tomorrow.

DECIDE YOUR DESTINY

My friend, Kyle Spyrides, is a perfect example of the body's ability to heal. At eighteen, he dreamed of becoming a professional rugby player but one night, after walking home from the gym, he felt an intense chill and had to wrap himself in blankets. Then, just as suddenly, he became burning hot. The next night he collapsed. He was fully conscious but unable to move.

Within days he was in a coma with all his organs shutting down and, in his words, "a 3cm bug eating into my heart." When Kyle came out of the coma a week later, he was told he needed surgery immediately and would be on medication for the rest of his life. The doctors also gave him only a 33% chance of surviving surgery.

His stepfather, a chiropractor with years of experience, believed Kyle was too weak to survive the operation and told Kyle he had a choice: he could have surgery or he could rebuild his body first. He chose to rebuild his body. Together with his stepfather he studied nutrition, changed his diet, and created an internal environment where the infection couldn't survive.

Kyle spent his nineteenth birthday in hospital, but in time he became strong enough to have his heart valve repaired. He has now written an inspiring book called *Decide Your Destiny* and says: "There's something really empowering and satisfying and fulfilling in life when you feel like you're actually taking part in your life. You're not beholden to something else and you get to decide your destiny."

REBUILD YOUR BODY

If you're feeling exhausted or burned out, remember that you don't have to feel like this forever. You can change. You can start creating your new body today. How? By eating to build your body, one meal at a time. And it's easier than you think. Let's go through it step-by-step.

STEP 1: EAT LOTS OF GOOD FOOD – AND I MEAN LOTS!

This first step sounds simple, yet it never ceases to amaze me how many people don't eat enough good food. Many of my patients come to me because they can't lose weight, have hormonal problems, or feel exhausted all the time. And when we sit down together and go through what they eat, I see the same pattern over and over: they're under-eating.

Here's a common example of what people eat when they're trying to be "healthy" (do you see yourself in this daily diet?):

o Breakfast: a piece of toast or granola, low-fat yoghurt and fruit
o Lunch: a sandwich or salad and some fruit
o Dinner: a few vegetables or salad and a piece of meat, or maybe some pasta.

At first glance, this doesn't look unhealthy - no pizza, chips, or chocolate here. You might even feel proud if you ate like this every day. But here's the problem: you can't sustain this long-term without developing cravings, energy crashes, or mood swings.

Why not?

Take a moment to think of your body as a car. If you don't put fuel in, it's going to stop working. Simple as that. And it's the same with your body. You need to fuel it. And you need to fuel it well.

Let's look at that daily diet again. The cereal, vegetables, salads, fruit, bread, pasta all provide carbohydrates to fuel the body. That's great – so you have some energy to keep going.

However, where are the proteins? Proteins are the building blocks of your body. Your muscles, heart, liver, lungs – none of these can function properly without protein. If you're not eating enough of it, how can your body do what it's meant to do?

And if protein builds your body, what about fats? What role do they play? Quite a big one, actually. Your nerves are wrapped in a layer of fat called the myelin sheath. It's essential for transmitting nerve impulses. And your reproductive hormones - oestrogen, progesterone, and testosterone - are steroid-based, meaning they're made from fat.

So where do these essential proteins and fats come from? Only from what you eat.

STEP 2: CREATE A MEAL PLAN

"Before anything else, preparation is the key to success"
- Alexander Graham Bell

I cannot emphasise enough how important meal planning is in improving your health, especially if you're struggling with brain fog and fatigue.

How often do you open the pantry, find nothing healthy to snack on, and reach for a biscuit or a packet of chips? How often do you feel too tired to cook and end up ordering takeout? Or how often do you drag yourself to the supermarket, stare blankly at the shelves, forget what you meant to cook, and walk out with a ready-made meal you know is full of junk?

I've found the quickest way to plan meals is by using a simplified version of Robb Wolf's Paleo Matrix. I've adapted it to make it easier - especially if you're dealing with fatigue - and I recommend creating separate matrices for breakfast, lunch, and dinner.

I'll talk you through how to create the matrix, and then you'll find an example of it on the following page.

- o Take a piece of paper and divide it into three columns.
- o Label the columns:
- o Favourite carbohydrates
- o Favourite proteins
- o Favourite fats
- o Under each column, write down at least five healthy foods you genuinely enjoy from that food group (you'll find examples in the Simple Food Guide at the back of this book).
- o Once you've got your list, draw a line from one carbohydrate to one protein to one fat. That's your first meal!

You'll notice I haven't included a column for vegetables or salads because I want you to eat them with every meal. For now, aim for two cups of vegetables or salad per meal and try to vary them. Later in the book we'll talk more about how fruit and vegetables support your brain and hormones.

Keep drawing lines to mix and match until you have seven days' worth of meal ideas. If money is tight, choose just three foods per column and prepare them in different ways. That way, you can shop in bulk and less often.

Meal Matrix Example

Carbohydrates	Proteins	Fats
Sweet potato Brown rice Quinoa Sourdough bread Oats	Chicken Eggs Salmon (tinned or fresh) Tofu or tempeh Full-fat yoghurt	Avocado Olive oil Nuts or seeds Butter or ghee Oily fish

Now, mix and match by choosing one item from each list to build a balanced meal. Don't forget to add in two cups of vegetables or salad. For example:

- o **Breakfast**: Oats + Full-fat yoghurt + Nuts or seeds + Banana
- o **Lunch**: Brown rice + Tinned salmon + Olive oil + Vegetables
- o **Dinner**: Sweet potato + Chicken + Avocado + Salad

You now have the foundation for a day of nourishing meals. You can repeat this process to create a full week's worth of ideas.

STEP 3: PLAN YOUR SHOPPING

Once you've created your seven-day meal plan, write out a shopping list of all the ingredients you'll need and take a photo of it with your phone. I say this because, if you're anything like me, you'll get to the shops and realise you've forgotten the list! Then you'll end up buying everything *except* what you actually need. Am I right? If the list is saved on your phone, you'll have it with you when you need it.

STEP 4: ASK FOR HELP

When I chat to my patients with fatigue, I'm reminded how hard the little, everyday things like cooking and shopping can be. So please, don't be afraid to ask for help.

Ask other members of your household to help with the planning, shopping and cooking. You don't have to do it all yourself. One of the best things I ever did was ask my husband to take over the supermarket shopping. I never enjoyed it, and I usually forgot the list anyway!

If you live alone, ask a friend or family member for support. Or try shopping online and having your groceries delivered. You could also use a meal delivery service for a few weeks. Your priority is simple: get regular, nourishing food into your body and start building steady, supportive routines.

SOME FINAL TIPS

Keep it simple and easy

Eating to build your body is essential for restoring your health and energy but I know how hard it is to put that into practice when you're running on empty.

So, make it easy for yourself. Buy ready-cooked meats, pre-washed and chopped vegetables, or ready-made salads from your supermarket. You don't need to be a domestic god or goddess to be healthy. You don't have to do everything yourself or do it perfectly. Right now, your only job is to nourish your body and rest.

For example, if you've got no energy at night, pick up a cooked chicken and a bag of pre-chopped roast vegetables. Pop the vegetables in the oven for half an hour, drizzle with olive oil, and hey presto dinner is ready! Delicious. Simple. Quick.

If you're serious about rebuilding your energy go and lie on the couch while the vegetables roast. Just rest. Do nothing else.

Lunches can be tricky, especially if you're working. To make things easier, either cook extra dinner and save some for the next day or do a big Sunday cook-up. One of my patients cooks twelve egg muffins every Sunday morning and freezes them. That's six healthy work lunches made in only half an hour.

I know many health professionals discourage eating leftovers and I know pre-cut vegetables cost a little more. But if you're struggling with fatigue, you need to make allowances for yourself. Do what saves you energy and time because right now those are precious. Within a few weeks of eating to balance your blood sugars and build your body, you'll start to feel better. With more energy, you'll feel like you have more time and when you're ready, you'll be able to do more.

Start Where You Are

As you progress through this book you will be asked to make bigger, more difficult changes to your diet and learn more 'rules' for eating for energy. For now, don't change too much too quickly, don't give up all the foods you love and don't try to eat 'super-healthy' foods which you don't enjoy. If you do these all you'll be doing is adding more stress to your life which is not what you need.

Instead, start with small, easy changes. Stick with them for a few weeks until they become part of your daily routine and after a while you'll notice you have more energy to make the bigger, harder changes.

For now, don't overhaul your diet. Simply make these two small adjustments:

- o **Include a healthy protein and/or fat with every meal and snack.** This helps balance your blood sugar and gives your body what it needs to rebuild.
- o Aim for two cups of fresh vegetables or salad with every meal to support energy, digestion, and overall nourishment.

Make Friends with Salt

Although salt is seen as the bad guy in so many health conditions, when it comes to fatigue and low energy, salt is your friend. As long as you don't use too much, and you use a good quality salt such as unrefined sea salt or Himalayan pink salt. These salts contain trace minerals that support your adrenals, thyroid and nervous system and will help raise your blood pressure a little if you're feeling light-headed or dizzy.

Don't Jump on The Health-Food Ferris Wheel

One mistake I often see in people struggling with their health is them replacing a natural, varied diet with health trends such health bars, health bombs, green drinks, or bulletproof coffee. This approach isn't sustainable, it can get expensive, and many of these products are high in sugar (even if its natural sugar).

I truly believe the best and healthiest way to eat is simple: a varied, natural diet made up of homecooked meals and whole foods.

5, Eat To Calm the Fire

Think of a special friend. Now imagine their house is on fire and you're standing outside, holding a hose connected to an endless supply of petrol. Would you aim it at the flames? Pour petrol onto the fire? I doubt it. Yet, chances are, you're doing exactly that to yourself right now.

Let me explain.

Imagine your body is a house on fire. It's burning down and edging closer to collapse. You've called the firemen, and they're doing their best to put the flames out but for some reason, the fire just keeps burning. The heat and smoke are so intense that you can't see clearly enough to work out where it all began.

Then you look down and see you're holding a hose. And it's not spraying water - it's spraying petrol. You're feeding the fire instead of extinguishing it. No wonder the firemen can't get it under control.

This is what I see often in people struggling with fatigue and it might be happening to you. The burning house is your body. The firemen are the therapies, herbs, or supplements you keep turning to in an effort to feel better. The petrol is the food you eat, the habits you keep, and the ways you push through when your body is telling you to stop. And the flames? The flames are a physiological process known as chronic inflammation.

If you're still pouring petrol onto the fire, the firemen can't succeed. Before anything else, you need to stop feeding the flames and cool the inflammation.

WHAT IS CHRONIC INFLAMMATION?

Do certain foods leave you bloated or crampy? Do you get frequent skin rashes, postnasal drip, or mouth ulcers? What about sore joints after exercise, headaches, brain fog, or trouble concentrating? Perhaps you struggle with allergies like hay fever, eczema, or sinus issues?

All of the above have one thing in common: chronic inflammation.

Inflammation is your body's natural response to injury. Think of what happens when you twist an ankle or get stung by a bee: there is swelling, redness, heat and pain. This is acute inflammation and is your immune system stepping in to protect and heal.

Sometimes this inflammation doesn't switch off. It settles in and affects your entire body in a low-grade, ongoing way, damaging your body instead of healing or protecting it. This is chronic inflammation.

While acute inflammation is obvious and easy to spot, chronic inflammation isn't. It doesn't come with visible swelling or redness. Instead, it quietly causes aches and pains, fatigue, poor sleep, mood swings, digestive problems or frequent colds and infections. With these vague symptoms it's easy to miss and it can go on to contribute towards long-term conditions like asthma, heart disease, diabetes, obesity, anxiety, depression, and even dementia.

If you're struggling with fatigue, there's a good chance chronic inflammation is playing a role. It's important to identify not just what may have caused it, but also how you're continuing to fuel it day after day.

I often find that the original cause of inflammation is quite different from what's keeping it going. Like a house fire started by faulty wiring, a candle, or a dropped cigarette, it might begin one way but continue because someone keeps throwing on petrol, wood, or twigs.

What is quite frightening with chronic inflammation, is that it's usually our lifestyle that feeds the inflammation and stops us from getting well. Our daily habits become the fuel, blocking recovery and keeping us stuck. The way we eat, move, and handle stress doesn't just lead to burnout; it keeps us there.

DO YOU HAVE A 'BIG BELLY'?

Strange question, I know - but hear me out. If you've been struggling with fatigue for a while, you may have noticed weight gain that's hard to shift. If that extra weight is sitting around your waist while the rest of your body remains relatively slim, it's something to pay attention to because it's a sign of chronic inflammation.

Chronic inflammation causes fat to accumulate specifically around the waistline. At the same time, excess fat around the waist triggers inflammation. In other words, chronic inflammation leads to belly fat and belly fat fuels chronic inflammation. Do you see where I'm going with this? It's a vicious cycle.

Chronic inflammation is also linked to obesity through two key hormones: leptin and insulin. These hormones play essential roles in how our bodies use energy, but both these hormones also promote inflammation and weight gain. If you're overweight and have fatigue then it will be difficult for you to lose weight, but not impossible.

It's important to reduce this belly fat and fad diets won't help. What will help is lowering inflammation by following the steps I outline in this book. Don't eat to control your weight, rather eat to dampen your inflammation. You'll find that as the inflammation decreases your weight will naturally decrease.

Over the next few chapters, we'll explore some of the causes and fuels of chronic inflammation. Take your time working through them and make just one change to your diet or lifestyle at a time. Don't try to implement everything at once. It won't be sustainable. Instead, take your time and make gradual adjustments at a pace that feels right for you.

WHAT ARE YOU EATING?

One of the easiest places to start is by swapping out processed foods and drinks for natural, whole foods. Processed products fuel the fire of inflammation to such an extent that I recommend you clear them out of your kitchen today and stop eating them for good.

So if you're ready to start feeling better, take this book with you into your kitchen, grab a bin bag, and clear out:

- o **All processed proteins** such as ham, polony, salami, bacon, processed cheeses, ready-made meals, and fast foods
- o **All processed fats** such as polyunsaturated cooking oils, margarine, shortening, mayonnaise and low-fat sweetened dairy products
- o **All processed drinks** such as sodas, packaged cappuccinos and instant hot chocolates.

From now on, aim to eat foods in their most natural, whole form and:

- o **Swap out processed proteins** for eggs, seeds, nuts, wild-caught fish, grass-fed meats, and free-range full-cream dairy
- o **Replace processed fats** with cold-pressed oils like olive, avocado or macadamia oil
- o **Choose fresh** juice, filter coffee, or homemade hot chocolate over packaged drinks.

I know this way of eating can be more expensive, but if you want to feel better and have the energy to enjoy life, eating well is essential. Stop feeding your body foods that inflame you and damage your health.

FATS – THE GOOD, THE BAD AND THE UGLY

As you saw in the list above, I recommend throwing out all processed fats - I call these the "bad" fats. But there are also "good" fats that are essential to our health. I want to take a moment to talk about both, as there's still a lot of confusion around them.

Not long ago, fat had a bad reputation. It was linked to heart attacks, high blood pressure and early death. It still is, but we now know that certain fats are crucial to good health. For instance, did you know your brain is 60% fat? Or that some of your hormones are made from fat? Good fats are vital for growth, metabolism, immunity, reproduction and mental health. Our bodies can't make them on their own so we need to get them from our diet. Let's take a closer look at the fats we eat.

Dietary fats come in different forms:

- o **Saturated fats** are found in animal foods like meat, eggs, butter, and cream, as well as tropical oils like coconut oil. These fats provide energy and are generally safe when eaten in moderation. They're also heat-stable, making them suitable for cooking.
- o **Monounsaturated fats** are vital to good health. They're found in plant sources such as nuts, seeds, extra virgin olive oil and even in olives. Use them raw or in low-heat cooking as they're less stable at high temperatures.
- o **Polyunsaturated fats** are liquid at room temperature. Some are good for you and some are bad for you – it can get quite confusing!
- o Avoid vegetable seed oils such as sunflower, canola, corn, soy and safflower oils as well as margarines, store-bought

salad dressings and many prepackaged or ready meals. These fats will inflame your body.

- o Eat plenty of oily fish, seeds and nuts. They're anti-inflammatory and your brain loves them!
- o **Trans fats or partially hydrogenated fats** are used in restaurants and fast-food venues for frying, making snacks etcetera. They are highly inflammatory and wreak havoc on your body. They're 'ugly' fats and should be completely avoided.

Take a moment today to go through your pantry and fridge and clear out any bad fats you find. Toss them in the bin. It's a small but important step toward getting your energy back. Every time you eat deep-fried chips or pour store-bought dressing over a salad, you're pouring fuel onto that fire!

Throw away:

- o Canola, corn, soy, sunflower, safflower oils
- o Margarine and shortening
- o Store-bought mayonnaise and salad dressings
- o Deep-fried foods
- o Processed meats and cheeses.

Replace with:

- o Butter, ghee, or coconut oil for cooking
- o Cold-pressed oils (olive, avocado, macadamia) for salads
- o Homemade mayo and dressings
- o Oven-baked alternatives
- o Natural, home-prepared meals.

DO YOU HAVE AN UNDERLYING INFECTION?

In Chapter 2, I listed common causes of fatigue your doctor can easily rule out like anaemia, hypothyroidism, and obvious infections.

Now, let's look at less obvious infections that may not directly cause fatigue but can contribute to it by triggering chronic inflammation or weakening the immune system.

A high percentage of patients who come to me with fatigue have had a previous infection, often as a teenager. Infections such as glandular fever and traveller's diarrhoea are the most common.

Although they may no longer have symptoms of an active infection, what these patients all have in common is that their immune systems are still mounting an inflammatory response, sometimes to something that happened years ago. In other words, they've developed chronic inflammation.

James's case is a perfect example of how a hidden infection can result in fatigue. When he first came to see me, he had black circles around his eyes, became breathless when talking, experienced night sweats, and felt completely drained for two to three days after any exercise. He was only in his early twenties and until a year ago, was fit and athletic, surfing regularly and training in the gym.

Two years previously he had been on holiday in Bali and picked up "traveller's diarrhoea". He recovered on his own and felt fine after returning home to South Africa. Then he settled into a new training routine that included three to four hours a day in the gym and one day he just crashed. He lost all his energy, his joints swelled and hurt, his throat and ears constantly ached and he became breathless just walking up the stairs.

Suspecting the traveller's diarrhoea may have triggered his fatigue, I started my investigations with a stool test. It showed he had a parasitic infection, even though he had no obvious digestive symptoms. Once we knew what we were dealing with, I was able to treat him with antiparasitic herbs and homoeopathic remedies.

Much to his horror, I also suggested he scale back his exercise for the next three months. Instead of gym workouts and runs, I recommended gentle walks, slow swims, yin or restorative yoga, and breathing exercises. While movement is essential for good health, pushing too hard when your body is inflamed or fighting an infection can do more harm than good. It only adds fuel to the fire. Sometimes the best thing you can do is rest and give your body the time it needs to heal.

Here is a list of the most common infections that are associated with fatigue. Some of these are endemic to a particular region so you do need to tell your doctor your travel history just in case you picked up one of these infections whilst away from home. For example, if you live in the United Kingdom, there is minimal chance of your doctor testing you for Ross River virus unless you specifically ask. However, if you've travelled to Australia or some of the South Pacific islands then there is a chance you may have contracted it and it could be adding to your fatigue.

Ask your doctor to run the necessary tests to rule these out:

- o Epstein–Barr virus (EBV)
- o Cytomegalovirus (CMV)
- o Human herpesvirus 6 (HHV-6)
- o Parvovirus B19
- o Ross River virus (RRV)
- o Mycoplasma spp.
- o Borrelia burgdorferi or mayonii (Lyme disease)
- o Coxiella burnetii (Q fever)
- o Histoplasma spp.
- o Candida spp.
- o *Schistosoma* spp. (bilharzia)

Also, as recommended in Chapter 2, visit your dentist. Dental abscesses are not always painful or noticeable and can contribute to chronic inflammation without you being aware of them.

For some of these infections there's currently no known medical treatment. However, and this is why I love homoeopathy, there's a group of homoeopathic remedies called nosodes that can support the body in recovering from the long-term effects of past infections. If you test positive for any of the infections listed above, consider seeing a qualified homoeopathic doctor who can guide you through the next steps.

HAVE YOU HAD AN INJURY OR OVER-EXERCISED?

I've noticed that some patients with fatigue haven't had an infection, but did, at some point, experience an accident, major injury, or surgery and they've never felt well since.

For reasons we don't always fully understand, the body sometimes doesn't recover properly after an injury, surgery, or even intense exercise, and chronic inflammation can set in. This might be because physical trauma affects more than just muscles and bones - it also impacts the nervous system. Sometimes the body stays "stuck" in a stress response long after the injury has healed. When that happens, the nervous system remains on high alert, making it hard for the body to truly rest and repair. Over time, this constant tension can drain energy and slow down healing.

It could also be due to the natural inflammatory response your body launches after any physical trauma, whether it's a fall, a torn muscle, or repeated micro-damage from exercise. Inflammation is part of the healing process, and it's helpful at first. But if it doesn't settle down, it can linger in the background, quietly fuelling fatigue.

Some bodyworkers believe that injuries leave a kind of imprint in our connective tissue (fascia), and if that tension isn't released, it may interfere with energy flow and circulation. This idea is still being explored, but it's an interesting layer to consider when looking at long-term fatigue.

So if you've been tired for a while, take a moment to reflect: Did your symptoms begin after an injury, surgery, or a period of heavy training?

When considering this, be aware not all injuries are obvious and many people overlook the impact of over-exercising. My husband laughs at me when I get onto this topic because I'm always looking for an excuse not to exercise. But the truth is, too much exercise without enough recovery can trigger inflammation.

The good news is, this kind of inflammation can be eased through the lifestyle changes I share in this book, as well as with homoeopathic remedies and herbal medicine.

ARE YOU BEING EXPOSED TO MOULD OR MYCOTOXINS?

Chronic exposure to mould - whether at home, at work, or through contaminated food - can also contribute to inflammation. Research on the topic is mixed, and it's one of those chicken-and-egg situations: does exposure to mould and other airborne microbes trigger chronic inflammation, or are you simply more sensitive to them because you're already inflamed?

Whatever the answer, living or working in damp, poorly ventilated environments increases your risk of exposure to airborne pollutants. Over time, these aggravate an allergic-type inflammatory response that contributes to fatigue. So, it's important to check your home and workplace for any signs of water damage or mould. If you find any, get professional help to fix it.

Moulds are not only a problem in your home. They also grow on a variety of crops and foodstuffs and produce toxic compounds called mycotoxins. Several hundred different mycotoxins have been identified so far. The most well-known are aflatoxins which can be found in some cereal crops such as corn, wheat and rice; oilseeds such as sunflower or soybean; spices such as black pepper, coriander and ginger; and tree nuts like almonds, walnuts or pistachios.

I think you would drive yourself mad if you tried to avoid every type of food on which mould could possibly grow but you can try to reduce your exposure to mycotoxins by eating a wide range of different foods, buying grains and nuts as fresh as possible, and not storing these types of food for too long.

WHICH CAME FIRST: THE CHICKEN OR THE EGG?

No one truly knows what causes ongoing, severe fatigue. For some people, it begins after an infection, injury, or surgery. It's easy to say the infection triggered the fatigue but, at the same time, we have to ask why they didn't recover. Why do some people bounce back from something like traveller's diarrhoea, while others are left with years of debilitating exhaustion? Take Epstein-Barr virus (EBV), for example. More than 90% of people worldwide carry it. So why do some EBV-positive people go on to develop chronic fatigue, while others feel completely fine?

For others, fatigue creeps in slowly without them noticing until, after months or even years, they discover they have developed multiple food intolerances or a sensitivity to mould. Again, we could argue that it's the food that they're eating or the mould in their home that is causing their fatigue. Or we could ask ourselves why they're so sensitive to mould when no one else in their home is.

Do you see where I'm going with this? Which came first – the chicken or the egg?

It's human nature to blame one thing. To constantly look for the one cause of an illness. But deep fatigue is rarely that simple. It's complex, layered, entangled like a spider's web. You can't pull on just one strand and expect it all to come loose. You can't pinpoint one cause and assume you've solved it.

I've seen it time and again - someone struggles with fatigue for years, discovers mould in their home, removes it and feels much better. But a few months later, the exhaustion returns - this time triggered by a food intolerance. They eliminate the food, feel good briefly, then come down with an infection. And so, the cycle continues.

What I'm trying to say is this: Even if your doctor finds a specific infection and treats it successfully, it's still important to make the lifestyle changes I recommend in this book.

And more importantly, ask yourself: *Why is my body reacting so strongly?*

Instead of asking why you're sick, ask yourself why you're not healing.

In my experience, the answer to that question often lies in the emotional work I'll guide you through in Parts 3 and 4. I truly can't emphasise enough how much our mental and emotional health influences our physical wellbeing and our potential to heal.

6, LISTEN TO YOUR BODY

So far we've looked at the more obvious, external causes of inflammation. Now we're going to look at less obvious, more insidious causes. If you already eat a clean diet and live in a healthy environment yet still have fatigue, then hopefully this chapter will help you find some answers.

FOOD INTOLERANCES

The foods we eat either build our bodies or break them down. They either nourish us or inflame us. Unfortunately, it's not only the 'bad' foods that inflame us. Sometimes, for some people, it can be the 'good' ones too. Even healthy foods can cause an inflammatory response in our bodies if we're intolerant to them or if we have a leaky gut.

Food intolerances and leaky gut go hand-in-hand but to help you understand them better I'll talk about them separately.

We'll start with food intolerances but before we get into them, I want to clarify the difference between a food intolerance and a food allergy because they're not the same process and need to be treated differently.

Food allergies are not connected to fatigue or burnout. When you have an allergic reaction to a food, your body has an exaggerated immune response that involves an antibody called immunoglobulin E (IgE).

Antibodies are proteins made by your immune system to help it recognise and fight foreign substances. During an IgE-mediated response, a number of different inflammatory molecules, such as histamine, are released. Within seconds your mouth may start itching, and your throat, face, or other areas of your body might swell. You could develop a rash, have trouble breathing, or even vomit.

If you experience a reaction like this, it's vital to seek medical help immediately. The guidance in this book is not intended for managing food allergies.

A food intolerance, on the other hand, is usually less dramatic and, like chronic inflammation, can be hard to recognise. Symptoms are often vague, generalised, and may only appear 48 to 72 hours after eating the offending food. Symptoms may include:

- o Abdominal pain or cramps
- o Bloating and gas
- o Diarrhoea and/or constipation
- o Irritable bowel syndrome (IBS)
- o Reflux or heartburn
- o Headaches
- o Tiredness
- o Trouble concentrating
- o Brain fog
- o Joint pain or muscular aches and pains
- o Snotty nose
- o Post-nasal drip
- o Hives or urticaria
- o Skin rashes, dermatitis or eczema
- o Mouth ulcers.

Food intolerances are not IgE-mediated and can arise for several different reasons. For instance, if you're intolerant to milk, it might be because your body doesn't produce enough of the enzyme needed to break down lactose. Or it could be due to a hyper-permeable, or 'leaky', gut that allows larger food particles to enter the bloodstream and trigger a reaction.

The most common food intolerances include gluten, dairy, corn, soy, and eggs but a person can be intolerant to almost anything. Sometimes, you can spot patterns that help pinpoint the culprit. For example, if you have more mucous-related symptoms like post-nasal drip, a constantly runny nose, sinus congestion, or recurring ear infections, dairy may be worth eliminating. On the other hand, if your symptoms are more skin-related, for example frequent hives, facial flushing, or a persistently runny nose, then you might want to start by cutting out histamine-rich foods like aged cheese, cured meats, and citrus fruits.

However, it's not always possible to figure out exactly what you're intolerant to and food intolerances can be incredibly frustrating. I've seen many people feel like giving up on trying to get well because no matter how "healthy" their diet is, they still react to almost everything they eat.

If that's you - if you've cut out all your favourite foods but are still dealing with bloating, gas, pain, or if you've ditched dairy and gluten but still have eczema and feel constantly tired - then I recommend trying an elimination diet. It's a slow and sometimes difficult process, but it can be so worthwhile. You might even discover you can go back to enjoying your favourite cheese and ice cream again.

HOW TO DO AN ELIMINATION DIET

Elimination diets sound easy at first: all you need to do is keep a food diary for a while, look for any symptom patterns, give up the foods you suspect may be causing the symptoms and then reintroduce them one by one.

It sounds so simple, doesn't it? But believe me when I say it's easier said than done! I highly recommend you work together with a nutritionist or dietician if you want to do it properly. If you want to do it alone, then follow these steps below. Whatever you do, don't cheat because then you will need to start all over again!

STEP 1. KEEP A FOOD DIARY FOR 14 DAYS

For 14 days write down everything you eat and drink, including snacks, drinks, spices and condiments. Be sure to list every ingredient, for example don't just write "pasta and sauce" - note the type of pasta and what's in the sauce. Also record the day and time next to each food/drink entry.

At the same time, record any symptoms you notice during the day. For example, digestive issues such as bloating, cramping or reflux; mood or energy changes; brain fog or poor concentration; food cravings; skin rashes or itchiness; or any other symptoms that come up. Again, be sure to record the day and time next to each symptom entry.

STEP 2. REVIEW YOUR DIARY

After 14 days, review your diary. For every symptom you have recorded, look back over what you ate or drank in the 72 hours before it appeared. Look for which foods, drinks or ingredients show up repeatedly within the 72 hours before your symptoms appear. These are your "suspects". Make a list of all the suspects.

STEP 3. ELIMINATE THE SUSPECTS

This part can be hard, especially because we usually crave foods we're intolerant to. Try to remind yourself that all your hard work will be worth it in the end.

You now need to completely eliminate all the suspect foods from your diet. This means 100% elimination – no little treats or slip-ups.

Do not eat any of the suspects until your symptoms have improved. This usually takes two to four weeks.

Once all your symptoms have gone, continue avoiding the suspect foods for five more days. This gives you have a clear baseline so that you can challenge the suspects one by one. This is the next step.

STEP 4. CHALLENGE ONE FOOD AT A TIME

Once you've had five symptom free days you can start challenging the suspects. Make sure you only challenge one suspect at a time.

Restart your food diary and choose one food (only one!) from your suspect list to test. Eat that food for three days in a row:

- o   Day 1: Have a small amount
- o   Day 2: Eat a little more
- o   Day 3: Have a full portion.

Wait two full days without eating that food again. Watch for any symptoms and note them in your diary. If symptoms appear, then add that food to an "AVOID" list. If no symptoms appear, still avoid that food for now and test the next suspect.

Work your way through each food on your suspects list, one at a time.

STEP 5. AVOID ALL FOODS ON YOUR "AVOID" LIST

Hopefully there are only one or two foods on your "AVOID" list. Avoid eating these foods completely for three months.

This will be hard. You'll need to check labels, ask what's in sauces or meals when eating out or visiting friends, and stay aware of hidden ingredients. It will feel frustrating and restrictive but please remember, it's temporary.

You're not allergic to these foods; you're just intolerant to them at the moment. If you give your body time to settle and your gut time to heal, especially by following the protocol in the next chapter, there's a good chance you'll be able to enjoy these foods again. Just make sure you stick with it for the full three months, without slipping up, to give your body the best chance to reset.

Step 6. Reintroduce Foods One at a Time

After 3 months, reintroduce one food at a time. When reintroducing them, don't test an entire food group at once. Reintroduce one item at a time. For example, if you're testing dairy, start with just cheese. If that goes well, try cream. Then yoghurt. Then milk. Each food is different and I have many patients who can eat milk but not cream, or cream but not cheese etcetera.

The process of reintroducing foods is similar to that of challenging suspect foods:

- o Day 1: Eat a small amount
- o Day 2: Eat a little more
- o Day 3: Eat a full portion.

Watch for symptoms over the next 72 hours and note any changes in digestion, mood, energy, skin, etcetera. If no symptoms appear, you can begin eating that food again. If symptoms return, avoid the food for another 3 to 6 months and try reintroducing it again later.

———

Doing an elimination diet takes time and effort but it's worth it. Ask yourself: would you rather keep living with bloating, brain fog, and mouth ulcers? Or give up all your favourite foods indefinitely just in case one of them is the problem? Or would you rather spend a few focused weeks figuring out exactly which foods are causing your symptoms?

If you do discover an intolerance, it's a good idea to work with a qualified dietitian or nutritionist. One common mistake is cutting out the problematic food without replacing it with a proper alternative. Over time, this can lead to nutrient deficiencies and a range of other health issues.

7, HEAL YOUR GUT

You might've heard the term leaky gut and found yourself wondering, "What on earth is a leaky gut? How do I know if I have one? What can I do about it?" Or maybe you've brought it up with your doctor and had the whole idea dismissed or even laughed at.

The more technical terms for leaky gut are increased intestinal permeability or intestinal hyperpermeability. Although it's been talked about in natural health circles for a long time, it's only in the last few years that more solid research has begun to back it up in mainstream medicine, linking it to things like inflammation, autoimmune issues, and fatigue.

I'm going to share a little geeky science now, not to overwhelm you but to help you picture what's going on in your gut if you have increased permeability. Once you understand it, it will feel much easier to let go of the foods that may be making things worse.

A Look Inside Your Gut

When you start looking closely at your body, you'll be fascinated by its innate intelligence. Everything seems to have been created for a reason.

Estimates vary, but the surface area of your gut is surprisingly large, possibly up to 400m². It's covered in tiny folds and projections that help absorb nutrients and is designed to protect you, letting in what your body needs and keeping the rest out.

If you look closely at this lining, you'll discover it's a single layer of cells that absorb nutrients from your food and pass them into the bloodstream. These cells are lined by a thin layer of mucous and friendly microbes. Interconnecting the cells are tiny gatekeepers called tight junctions and they carefully control what gets through.

If these tight junctions are damaged, substances that were meant to stay inside your gut - like bits of undigested food, toxins, or bacteria - can leak into your bloodstream. Since these molecules don't belong in the blood, your immune system treats them as intruders and launches an inflammatory response. This can lead to low-grade, widespread inflammation, which might show up as sore joints, skin issues, fatigue, or other vague symptoms that are hard to pin down. It's your body's way of trying to protect you, but when this kind of inflammation becomes chronic, it gradually wears you down and affects your overall wellbeing.

We're still learning what damages these tight junctions, but a few things have been linked to problems. These include:

- o An imbalanced gut flora known as dysbiosis (something we'll explore in more depth shortly)
- o Eating foods that contain gliadin (like gluten)
- o Gut infections from parasites or fungi
- o High levels of ongoing stress
- o Serious physical trauma, like severe burns
- o Ageing.

You can test for leaky gut, but the tests can be expensive and, in most cases, I don't think they're necessary. The treatment approach is essentially the same as for addressing chronic inflammation, balancing your gut microbiome, and improving overall health: remove damaging foods, address any underlying infections, and eat in a way that supports healing. Whether or not you have a test confirming leaky gut, these are the steps your body needs. And honestly, running endless diagnostic tests can be exhausting, both emotionally and financially. Unless a test result is going to change your treatment plan, it may not be worth it. Also, if you suspect leaky gut, please don't lose heart. The cells lining your gut renew themselves every 3 to 5 days, which means your body is already trying to heal.

Here is a simple 3-step plan to help you start supporting this natural repair process and begin building a healthier gut in just a few weeks.

STEP 1: STOP EATING THOSE DAMAGING FOODS

Earlier I mentioned that some foods and additives can irritate a sensitive gut. Two groups often discussed are grains and emulsifiers. I'll explain each below.

GIVE UP GRAINS

If you choose to follow only one piece of advice from this entire book, please let it be giving up grains – don't panic, it's not forever!

I spent years trying different things to get my energy back, but nothing really shifted until I cut back on grains. Ironically, I didn't do it for myself - I did it to support my husband, who was trying to heal his Achilles tendonitis. He decided to go grain-free for 30 days, so I joined him.

I'd heard from patients and read articles about the benefits of giving up gluten, but I never thought it applied to me – I'm a 'tough Zimbabwean' raised on peanut butter sandwiches and I've never had digestive issues. Yet within the first two weeks of no grains, the brain fog I'd struggled with for years just lifted. I couldn't believe it.

If you struggle with fatigue, you'll know that feeling: a heavy head, a foggy brain, slow thinking. I'd always blamed my brain fog on stress, work, and burnout. But during those 30 days without grains, I didn't change anything else and the fog just lifted. My head felt clear for the first time in years. One of my patients who gave up gluten wrote to me saying: "The clarity in my head is just amazing. It's like a light went on."

A few weeks after the fog lifted, my memory started coming back. For years, I'd struggled to remember simple things like people's names or familiar places. You know that awful feeling when someone new walks up and you need to introduce a colleague… but their name just vanishes?

And yes, if you're wondering, my husband's tendonitis improved too!

Grains drain your energy and worsen fatigue in several ways - some are more obvious, and some are surprisingly hidden.

The Gluten Connection

Many people with fatigue are sensitive to gluten. The word *gluten* comes from the Latin word for "glue," which is why it's often called the *sticky protein*. Gluten helps bind foods and gives them elasticity - think of the stretchy texture of bread dough. Unfortunately, this same stickiness can interfere with the breakdown and absorption of other nutrients, and it's also been linked to damage of the gut's tight junctions.

Gluten is made up of two protein groups: gliadins and glutenins. A person can be sensitive to gluten as a whole or react to any one of the smaller units that make up these proteins. This is why some individuals experience symptoms when eating gluten, even though diagnostic tests show they don't have coeliac disease.

Dr David Perlmutter, a practising neurologist and pioneering researcher into neurodegenerative diseases, believes that gluten and high-carbohydrate diets are major drivers of inflammation in the brain. He says:

"Whether it's headaches and migraines, Tourette's syndrome, seizures, insomnia, anxiety, ADHD, depression, or just some odd set of neurological symptoms with no definite label, one of the first things I do is prescribe the total elimination of gluten from their diets. And the results continue to astound me."

Don't Go Gluten Free. Go Natural

Before going further, I want to emphasise something important here: *don't get caught up in the world of 'gluten-free' products.*

Gluten-free biscuits, muffins, pancakes, and breads can be costly and are often filled with refined starches, preservatives, and additives that don't support your health. Many of these products are made from ingredients like rice flour or tapioca starch, which spike your blood sugar quickly and leave you feeling drained rather than nourished.

Instead, focus on simple, natural options like potatoes, sweet potatoes and pseudo-grains such as quinoa, amaranth, and buckwheat. These whole foods provide fibre, vitamins, and minerals that give your body steady energy. You'll also find plenty of delicious grain-free recipes online - search for "paleo" recipes as a starting point.

And when it comes to bread, consider sourdough. If made traditionally, most of the gluten is broken down through fermentation, making it easier to digest and a healthier choice than most processed "gluten-free" loaves.

What About Lectins?

Whole grains are often high in plant proteins called lectins. In nature, lectins help plants defend themselves against pests and predators. But if in excess in the human body, they can interfere with mineral absorption and may bind to the gut lining, potentially triggering an inflammatory response.

If you're experiencing severe fatigue or dealing with an autoimmune condition, temporarily eliminating high-lectin foods might help ease your symptoms. Foods particularly high in lectins include whole grains, legumes, seeds and nuts.

That said, lectins aren't all bad. They also act as antioxidants and help stabilise blood sugar by slowing the digestion of carbohydrates. So it's neither necessary nor wise to eliminate them permanently. Instead, reduce or avoid them while your body heals, and then gradually reintroduce them as your symptoms improve.

Lectins are water-soluble and mostly found on the outer surface of foods. So when you reintroduce them to your diet soak them overnight and then rinse them and remove their outer skins before use. You can also try sprouting them.

The Hidden Chemical: Glyphosate

Many grain crops are sprayed with glyphosate, a widely used herbicide. In 2015, it was classified as a probable human carcinogen and has been linked to hormone disruption, liver and kidney issues, and a damaged gut microbiome.

I'll explain more about the microbiome soon, but for now, just know that anything affecting your gut flora can also affect your energy.

By cutting out grains - at least for a while - you're giving your body a break from foods that are commonly sprayed with glyphosate. If you choose to reintroduce grains to your diet, try to opt for organic varieties whenever you can.

Refined Carbs and Blood Sugar Crashes

Cutting back on grains also helps reduce refined carbohydrates and makes it easier to stabilise your blood sugars. Think about it: if you normally eat spaghetti bolognaise and drop the spaghetti, what can you add instead? More vegetables. If your afternoon snack is usually a muffin, what could you swap in? Maybe chicken, a boiled egg, or some avocado.

Without grains, you're more likely to reach for the good fats and proteins your body needs to heal. It really does make eating well that much easier.

Emulsifiers are additives used in processed foods to keep ingredients like oil and water mixed smoothly together. You'll find them in mayonnaise, ice cream, packaged sauces, baked goods, and non-dairy milks.

Emulsifiers damage the mucus that lines and protects your gut and disrupt the balance of your microbiome. This can lead to increased inflammation, leaky gut and changes in your metabolism.

STEP 2: TREAT ANY GUT INFECTIONS YOU HAVE

If you know, or suspect, you have a gut infection please see a health professional. I've met many people who've tried to treat themselves based on internet advice or tips from a health shop. They end up wasting time, money, and energy often without getting better. With proper testing and treatment targeted to the actual infection, they could have improved so much more quickly.

STEP 3: FEED AND NOURISH YOUR MICROBIOME

Lining your gut are trillions of tiny microorganisms that play a vital role in your health and wellbeing. These include bacteria, fungi, viruses, and protozoa - together known as your microbiota or gut flora. When we talk about these microbes along with all their genetic material, we call it the gut microbiome.

Your microbiome is central to your overall health. It supports mental health by producing neurotransmitters, vitamins, and other compounds that influence mood, focus, and emotional balance - for example, serotonin, GABA, BDNF, and even small amounts of vitamin B12. It also helps regulate blood sugar levels and hormones that control appetite, while acting as a gatekeeper for the tight junctions between your intestinal cells, protecting against leaky gut and chronic inflammation.

In addition, your microbiome breaks down and detoxifies harmful chemicals that may enter with food and interacts with millions of immune cells lining your gut, strengthening your defences and regulating inflammation. It ferments and digests compounds your digestive system can't process on its own. And finally, it helps regulate nutrient absorption, metabolism, and the overall function of your gut.

When you think about your own health - whether it's brain fog, anxiety, low mood, blood sugar problems, leaky gut, chronic inflammation, or low immunity - you can start to see how closely these challenges may be linked to the state of your microbiome.

Ideally, you and your gut microbes live in a balanced, mutually supportive relationship. Sometimes that balance gets disrupted, and the 'bad' microbes start to crowd out the 'good' ones. This is called dysbiosis.

The main causes of dysbiosis are:

o   A diet high in animal protein, sugar, and saturated (or 'bad') fats
o   Low fibre intake
o   Emulsifiers found in processed foods (like mayonnaise)
o   Artificial sweeteners
o   Foods sprayed with glyphosate (especially grains)
o   Frequent use of NSAIDs (like ibuprofen)
o   Jet lag and disrupted sleep-wake cycles.

Each of these can either damage your microbiome directly or shift the internal environment of your gut in a way that encourages imbalance.

If you're struggling with fatigue, chronic inflammation or a leaky gut, it's vital you start looking after your microbiome. Make it a priority!

Luckily, it's easier than you think, and you can start today. Start by cutting back on sugar and refined carbohydrates, eating more vegetables and adding fermented foods to your daily diet. Examples of fermented foods include, yoghurt (unsweetened, made with live cultures, full cream), sauerkraut, kimchi, kombucha and kefir. Try to include fermented foods and prebiotic foods with each meal, but don't stick to just one - rotate them to give your microbiome a variety of food.

Here are a few examples of how to eat to feed your microbiome:

- If you tolerate dairy, then try to eat live yoghurt regularly - have it for breakfast, make a dip with yoghurt and garlic, or use it in place of mayonnaise
- Drink kefir or kombucha
- Have tempeh instead of meat one night a week
- Enjoy a delicious miso soup
- Eat sauerkraut or pickles with your meals
- Try sourdough bread with a fermented cheese
- Cold potatoes are a wonderful prebiotic food. When they're cooked and then cooled they form resistant starch which your gut bacteria thrive on. Enjoy them as a potato salad, tossed with homemade mayonnaise or natural yoghurt for an extra nourishing meal.

If you're new to fermented foods, start slowly. Just a small amount each day is enough to begin with. Give your body time to adjust otherwise if you eat too much too quickly you may end up feeling very uncomfortable.

If you have digestive symptoms accompanying your fatigue - such as abdominal pain, bloating, flatulence, diarrhoea or constipation - then I suggest that you seek the help of a health professional before changing your diet too much. If you have dysbiosis, it often helps to start your healing journey with the protocol known as "Weed, Seed and Feed". Don't try to do this by yourself – rather find someone qualified to help you.

START HERE

I know these dietary changes can feel overwhelming. Just thinking about them can be exhausting and sometimes that alone is enough to stop you from starting. Yet I really urge you to give up grains. If you do so, you'll automatically be giving up refined carbohydrates.

Blood sugar imbalances are a common cause of energy crashes and mood swings. They're also stressful for your body. One of the main drivers of these imbalances is eating too many refined carbohydrates. Cutting out grains means you'll automatically reduce these.

If you're feeling unwell or run-down, it's time to eat in a way that builds your body, not just fuels it. Refined carbohydrates may give you quick energy, but they don't offer the raw materials your body needs to repair and rebuild. Healthy proteins and good fats do.

Chronic inflammation, which plays a major role in fatigue, is worsened by things like excess weight, food intolerances, and a leaky gut. Too many refined carbohydrates contribute to weight gain, and leaky gut is linked to gluten, lectins, and glyphosate - all commonly found in grains.

If you're struggling with leaky gut, then in addition to giving up grains, try adding free-range, organic bone broth to your diet. Bone broth is rich in collagen, amino acids, and minerals that will nourish and help repair your gut lining. You can drink it in place of tea or coffee, or you can add it to your stews and soups.

Alongside this, focus on plenty of healthy anti-inflammatory fats such as avocados, olive oil and coconut oil. These can calm inflammation and support the gut's natural healing process.

PART 2. EASE YOUR MIND

8, ARE YOU WORTH IT?

So far I've introduced some simple concepts on how to improve your health. I'm sure you're familiar with them: eat wholesome foods; make things easy for yourself; ask for help when you need it.

There's nothing complicated or costly here, but do you actually do these? Do you feed and nourish yourself with intention? Do you take the easier path when you can? Do you ask for help?

If you can honestly answer yes, then you probably don't need this book because you're probably not burned out. In all my years of working with people struggling with fatigue, I've never met a lazy person with burnout. Many people struggling with their energy are A-type personalities, achievers, doers, givers, helpers. People who don't have time to really look after themselves, who will always give more than 110%, who don't ask for help but are always ready to offer it.

Take my patient Martin, for example. His fatigue first started after he over-trained for a triathlon eight years ago. "I've never felt well since that race", he said. He finds he can't exercise anymore, has weekly migraines and insomnia. His doctor diagnosed him with chronic anxiety and a naturopath diagnosed him with adrenal fatigue.

Putting the labels aside, I asked Martin to tell me more about his life. He's had digestive issues and food intolerances since his teens. He got divorced ten years ago and told me he started doing triathlons during the most difficult years of his marriage. When I asked him about work, he laughed and said, "I'm a bit of a control freak, a perfectionist. Even at home everything must be perfect."

When I asked him about his childhood he closed up for a while and then told me his dad had been an abusive alcoholic and his mum had been very quiet, always trying to keep the peace and please his dad.

Martin's story is not unusual. When a new patient comes to me with an outer presentation of achievement, control, success, and perfectionism but describes an inner world of insomnia, anxiety, bad dreams, or chronic pain alarm bells go off.

Why is there such a mismatch between the outside and the inside? Why does someone so in control on the outside feel so chaotic within?

Often, when someone is a perfectionist or high achiever, there's a deeper story underneath. Usually a quiet but powerful belief that they're not enough. An intrinsic lack of self-worth. I know this because it's something I've struggled with myself for many years. If I'm honest, I'm still working on it.

NEVER GOOD ENOUGH

My dad's suicide left me with a void inside myself. An emptiness. Not growing up with a dad, I always felt I was missing something. I used to love spending time in my friends' homes where there was a dad in the house. That grounding, supportive energy of a father. My mum did remarry when I was ten years' old, but my stepdad was killed in a car accident a year later.

I think many kids who grow up in a single parent home feel this void, but I think the hole is immeasurably deep when your parent has either deserted you or been abusive towards you. You feel as if something is so very wrong with you. So wrong that your own parent chose to leave you or hurt you.

When I was young, I didn't think too much about my dad, but once I became a mum myself, once I had my own children, I began to struggle with the concept that my dad, through committing suicide, had purposely chosen to desert us children. When I held my own little girls in my arms, I felt such an overpowering need to protect them, love them, nurture them. I simply couldn't fathom hurting them or leaving them. If you're a parent, I think you'll know what I'm talking about.

It was around this time that my chronic fatigue really set in. I had this quiet, nagging voice asking: "Why wasn't I enough to make him stay?" And at the same time, another voice saying, "Grow up. Stop blaming your dad. It's been over 30 years." You know those internal arguments - the ones that loop around endlessly. The hurt six-year-old wanting to be seen. The adult trying to stay in control and move on.

I recently had a patient who told me her dad had been a violent alcoholic. She talked so serenely of him that I had to ask her how she managed to forgive him and move on.

She said it took her many years but through getting to know his life story and where he had come from, she had learned to accept him as he was. He was Polish and had been a prisoner of war in Dachau. He had tried to escape, been caught and shot in the leg. She said of him: "he was just doing the best he could with what he had." He simply wasn't equipped to be a warm, loving, gentle dad.

It was during this same period of my life, once I had become a mum, that I really started over-working. Pushing and extending myself far beyond what was healthy. At the time I didn't realise I was doing this. I was far too busy to even notice. I became the perfect example of who Brené Brown describes when she says, "We are a culture of people who've bought into the idea that if we stay busy enough, the truth of our lives won't catch up with us."

Martin is the same. So are many of my other patients who've burned themselves out by keeping themselves too busy to feel their pain.

START GOING WITHIN

Many of us carry our traumas and losses with us wherever we go, especially those we're ashamed of, or the ones that make us feel small and worthless. We carry them as if they're huge boulders on our backs. Heavy weights that we take wherever we go in life.

I hear this in the way my patients describe their fatigue: "my legs feel so heavy when I try to walk", "it's such an effort to do anything", "my head is heavy all the time", "my eyes are heavy", "going out and seeing my friends is a drag", "I feel as if the air is thick, like I'm walking through honey …it's so hard, so much effort".

These weights that we carry are so big and dark that we feel tiny compared to them. Insignificant. So, we overcompensate by keeping our external lives in perfect order. We push forward, keep busy and work hard to avoid looking within.

If you want to start shifting your energy, stop trying to control everything around you and go within. Focus on building your sense of self-worth until you can comfortably be yourself just as you are. Because you are enough just as you are.

I know this is easier said than done but you can do it. A powerful tool I've come across to help people do this is writing the Morning Pages.

THE MORNING PAGES

Writing the Morning Pages is a simple everyday practice of writing two or three pages by hand, first thing each morning. The writing is not meant to be neat, clever, or even read again. The idea is simply to empty your head and clear out the mental clutter.

I first came across them in Julia Cameron's beautiful book *The Artist's Way*. At the time, I thought I wanted to learn to paint, but what I found instead was this daily ritual that ended up changing my life. I must have done it every morning for about 3 years! By putting your thoughts and worries on paper before the day begins, you create room for clearer thinking and more energy.

Every morning, as soon as you wake up, handwrite two to three pages of whatever is in your head. Don't overthink it, just write. It might be "The sun is shining" or "I don't know what to write." It doesn't matter what comes out. You're not writing a journal or a story. You're simply clearing mental clutter.

Don't reread what you've written. Instead, tear up the pages and throw them away. Let it all go. The goal is to clear space inside you so you can begin to feel lighter.

There'll be days when you don't want to do your pages, when they irritate or frustrate you or you think you don't have time, but still do them anyway. This resistance is completely normal and part of the process.

One of my patients phoned me early one morning in a rage, saying he found them irritating and a waste of his time, that he had nothing to write. If you feel like this, that's great! Just keep writing! If you wake up one morning and have nothing to write, that's okay. Simply describe the stripes on your pyjamas or the sound of the car on the road outside.

Over time you will be surprised at what you write. One of my patients said she felt like she was 'vomiting' onto her page when she was writing. That's okay. Better out than in! Another patient said halfway one morning she started scribbling like an angry child. She was shocked by her own behaviour. Again, I say that's okay, better out than in.

I remember being a bit horrified by some of the stuff that poured out of me some mornings – stuff I didn't even know was inside. What I did notice was how my nightmares reduced and I started sleeping so much better.

You may find yourself crying or you may find yourself ripping up the pages in a fury. Some days you may find yourself laughing and others you'll feel bored. Whatever you experience, just remember – it's okay! Keep writing!

JOURNALLING

An alternative to the morning pages is simply journaling and there's no rules when it comes to journaling. All you need to do is sit down and write – get all that weight that you're carrying around and put it down on paper.

As author Ryan Holiday says:

"Just know that it may turn out to be the most important thing you do all day," because journaling is *"a few minutes of reflection that both demands and creates stillness. It's a break from the world. A framework for the day ahead. A coping mechanism for troubles of the hours just past."*

A Note on Resistance

It's completely normal to feel resistance to the Morning Pages or journalling. Many people tell me, *"I can't write,"* or *"I hate writing."* Often, that resistance comes from a deeper belief that they're not good enough, or that they're not worth the effort of sitting down with themselves. Trying something new and unfamiliar can stir up these feelings, yet it's often in this space of discomfort that change begins.

Remember, you don't have to be good at writing. These pages are not essays or stories, and no one will ever read them. They're simply a tool - a way of getting your thoughts, worries and emotions out of your head and onto paper. When you do, you will begin to release some of the heaviness you're carrying. You'll begin to feel lighter.

9, REBUILD YOUR SENSE OF WORTH

The Morning Pages and journalling will help you get to know yourself, warts and all. This is the first step in rebuilding your energy.

The second step is to start developing a sense of self-worth, a deep knowing that you're enough just as you are.

That you don't need to do any more, be any more or achieve anything more. You are enough. Full-stop.

Think about this: out of approximately 100 million sperm released during an ejaculation, only one is successful in fertilising a woman's egg. You are here right now. You beat all those other millions of sperms trying to make it to your mum's egg. You've done enough. You are worthy! Now just be you.

Over the next few pages, I'll share some simple exercises to help you build your sense of self-worth. They may feel a little strange or even pointless at first. That's perfectly normal. In fact, the more resistance you feel, the more likely the exercise is exactly what you need. As Henry Rollins once said, "Pain is not my enemy. It is my call to greatness. Learning about what you're made of is always time well spent."

Before we begin, I want to acknowledge something important: talking about self-worth can feel confronting. If you've spent years ignoring your own needs or believing you're not enough, these exercises may bring up discomfort. If that happens, don't let it discourage you. Take your time, pause when you need to, and come back when you're ready.

LOVE YOUR MIRROR

When Madeleine first walked into my office I was conscious that I was staring but I couldn't help myself - she was such a beautiful woman! You can imagine my surprise when she told me how ugly she felt and how desperate she was to look different.

I gave her an exercise that sounds simple but is surprisingly difficult: mirror work. For Madeleine, it felt impossible at first. We tried it together in my office but she just couldn't do it. I suggested she try it at home in private, at her own pace.

When she came to see me a month later something deep had shifted. Something had lifted. She told me she had kept trying the exercise every day. At first, she couldn't do it. Then, slowly, she could. It made her cry, yet she continued trying.

For a lot of people, mirror work is uncomfortable. For some people it is unbearable. For others, it is almost impossible. So here's an invitation. Put this book down. Go to a mirror. Look yourself in the eyes and say out loud:

"Hello gorgeous. I love you."

Can you say it? And mean it?

If you can't say it and mean it, then practise it daily until you can look yourself in the eye and see yourself with love and respect.

Popularised by Louise Hay in the 1980s, mirror work is a deceptively simple practice with a lot of psychological depth. Most of us avoid truly looking into our own eyes and when we do we tend to feel uncomfortable. Feelings of shame, self-criticism or the sense that we're not enough start to surface and it's easier to look away. Yet mirror work can interrupt this avoidance and gently force you to be with yourself. It's like exposure therapy: the more you see yourself, the more comfortable you become with yourself.

Saying positive words about yourself in the mirror challenges your inner critic. Many people carry inner voices - often shaped by childhood, culture, or painful experiences - that whisper, "You're not worthy." Speaking affirmations in the mirror challenges those voices head-on. It's harder to dismiss kind words when you are both the speaker and the receiver. Looking into your own eyes while saying, "I am worthy" simulates the experience of someone else offering you love and acceptance.

This practice can gradually help you build self-compassion and a healthier inner dialogue. It blends thought with feeling, logic with emotion. Instead of simply telling yourself you "should" feel confident, you begin to feel it. Over time, the brain rewires, associating your reflection with kindness and worth rather than criticism or indifference.

That is how mirror work shifts from being uncomfortable at first to becoming a daily reminder of your inner worth.

PRACTISE STILLNESS

Sitting quietly, taking a breath, meditating - I like to call it practising stillness.

You probably already know how good meditation can be for you. Maybe you've even wanted to start a practice but haven't had the time or energy to make it stick. Or perhaps you've tried once or twice and felt like it just didn't work for you.

Starting to meditate can be frustrating. It can leave you feeling like you've failed or like you've added another task to your already overwhelming to-do list. Another pressure. Another expectation.

Rather than trying to meditate perfectly, I invite you to try Alan Watts's approach: just sit for a while and be still. Don't do anything else.

This is how he describes it in *The Watercourse Way*:

"You are asked – temporarily, of course – to lay aside all your philosophical, religious, and political opinions, and to become almost like an infant, knowing nothing...

Let your ears hear whatever they want to hear; let your eyes see whatever they want to see; let your mind think whatever it wants to think; let your lungs breathe in their own rhythm.

Do not expect any special result, for in this wordless and idealess state, where can there be past or future, and where any notion of purpose?

Stop, look, and listen...and stay there awhile before you go on reading."

I like to think of this approach as creating 'bubbles of stillness' and it's something I try to do throughout my day. For example, before I start work in the morning I make a coffee and sit on my garden bench for a few quiet minutes. I listen to the birds, stroke my cat and let my mind wander. When my coffee is finished, I get up and get on with my day. It's such a small, simple routine but it feels like a gift each day.

What small gift can you give yourself? If you work in an office, take your lunch outside. Find a bench in the sunshine and enjoy the busyness of the city, knowing that for the next five minutes you don't need to do a thing.

Do this not because you've earned it but because you're worth it. Practise stillness regularly. The more you practise it, the more you'll enjoy it.

BE YOUR OWN BEST FRIEND

Many people struggle with not feeling good enough. Some try to fill that void with clothes, cars, or changing their appearance. Those with burnout often try to earn their worth by helping others, staying busy, or achieving more.

But giving from an empty place only leads to deeper exhaustion.

To truly restore your energy, you need to build an inner sense of 'enoughness.' This takes time and begins with treating yourself with the same care you'd offer someone you love.

Take a moment to picture a special friend of yours. Would you want them to do everything perfectly, never ask for help, or eat unhealthy food all the time? Probably not.

So why treat yourself that way?

Research shows us that treating ourselves with the same kindness we'd show a friend reduces stress, supports emotional regulation, and builds a healthier sense of self-worth. In contrast, constant self-criticism is linked to anxiety, depression, and burnout.

So start caring for yourself as if you are caring for a special friend. Follow the simple steps from earlier chapters: eat to balance your blood sugar and build your body; keep meals and shopping easy; and ask for support when you need it.

Every nourishing meal, every moment of rest, every time you accept help you're sending yourself the message: I am worthy. Treat yourself as you would someone you love.

Before You Go

As you come to the end of this chapter, I want you to take a moment to ask yourself some painful questions. Take out your journal so you can record the answers and one day look back at them:

Why am I always busy?

Why do I keep pushing myself even when I'm tired?

Why do I believe I need to keep *doing, doing, doing* in order to be enough?

These questions aren't meant to judge or shame you, they're here to open a door.

I want you to know that you don't need to earn your worth through productivity or perfection. You already are enough, exactly as you are.

Let this be your mantra: "I am enough. I am worthy." Stand in front of your mirror and say it every day until it becomes your truth.

10, The Stress That Never Sleeps

Stress is a tricky thing to write about. It's so deeply personal that while it creates specific physiological changes in the body, the experience of it is different for each of us.

One person's stressful childhood might build resilience while another's might lead to lifelong anxiety, depression, or illness. Work stress might give you headaches and high blood pressure, it might flare up your gut, skin, or immune system, or it might drive you to work harder. We all react differently.

In this chapter, I'm not going to go into the physiology of stress in any depth. Instead, I want to help you explore your own stressors, whatever they may be.

Stressors set off a chain reaction in your body to help you survive. Fascinatingly, the body responds in a similar way whether the stress is emotional, physical, or chemical. Whether it's a lion chasing you, your boss yelling, or a blood sugar crash, it all sets off the same survival mode: hormones surge, energy is redirected, blood sugar changes, and your body gets ready to fight, freeze, flee or fawn.

The main hormones behind a stress reaction are adrenaline (epinephrine), noradrenaline (norepinephrine), and cortisol. When under stress, adrenaline and noradrenaline are like the match that sparks a fire. They flare up in seconds, giving you an instant burst of energy, a racing heart, and sharp focus so you can react right away.

Cortisol is more like the log on the fire. It takes a little longer to catch, but once it does, it keeps the stress response burning steadily, fuelling you for as long as the stress lasts. But if the fire is left burning too long, the fuel eventually dies down and cortisol levels fall, leaving you feeling flat and exhausted.

While this stress fire is blazing, your body diverts its fuel to survival and puts other systems on hold. Digestion, reproduction and long-term repair get starved of energy, which is why chronic stress so often shows up as digestive issues, menstrual problems, or fertility struggles.

LIFE'S LITTLE STRESSORS

We tend to focus a lot of our time and energy on coping with life's major stressors such as work, financial or family stress. Sometimes these stressors are beyond our control and this stresses us even more. It also tires us out.

If you're stuck in a highly stressful job that you really dislike yet have a mortgage to pay and a family to feed, you may feel you have no option but to stay. This sense of having no choice, of being unable to change your situation, adds to the stress you're already experiencing at work.

If you have a troubled teenager who you can't seem to help, no matter how hard you try, that lack of control only adds to the stress your child is already causing.

It's the same with finances. That sinking feeling of looking at an empty bank account each month is made worse when you feel powerless to change it.

We'll talk more about these 'big' stressors soon. Before we do, I want to introduce to you the idea of starting with what you can control.

There are plenty of small, everyday stressors I call *Life's Little Stressors*. They might seem minor - like running late, a cluttered desk, or a constantly buzzing phone - but your body still treats them as stress. Your adrenal glands still release stress hormones, and your nervous system still adjusts your heart rate, blood pressure, and blood sugar in response.

You might think these stressors are irrelevant, but your body still has to respond and that uses up energy. If you can reduce even a few of them, you'll free up more capacity to handle the bigger ones. As Charles Comiskey said, "It is the small things in life which count; it is the inconsequential leak which empties the biggest reservoir."

WHAT ARE YOUR LITTLE STRESSORS?

Start by looking at your environment. Some stressors, like noise and air pollution, hide in plain sight but we're so used to them we don't notice them.

Constant background noise (traffic, sirens, barking dogs, construction) can trigger a stress response and raise your blood pressure without you even realising it. Research links it to diverse health conditions ranging from heart disease to sleep disorders, so make a little time today to minimise unnecessary noise:

- o   Silence phone notifications
- o   Turn off TVs when you're not watching them
- o   Keep windows and doors closed if you live near busy roads
- o   Use heavy curtains, rugs, and carpets to dampen sound
- o   Add indoor plants to absorb noise
- o   Try earplugs or noise-cancelling headphones if necessary.

Polluted air, both indoors and out, also adds to your body's stress burden. Even common household items can contribute. Walk through your house and office and:

- o   Replace toxic cleaners with natural alternatives
- o   Use houseplants to freshen and filter your air

- o   Use a HEPA-filter vacuum to trap dust and allergens
- o   Clean your air-con filters regularly
- o   Consider an air purifier if needed.

Another source of daily stress can be your eating habits. Hopefully by now, you've started focusing on eating in a way that balances your blood sugars and nourishes your body. Hunger, nutrient deficiencies, and blood sugar ups-and-downs are all stressors for your system. In fact, every time your blood sugar drops too low, your body triggers the same stress response it would if a lion were chasing you.

LIFE'S BIG STRESSORS

Some of life's bigger stressors leave us feeling overloaded and helpless because they're so beyond our control. Yet our stress response is actually shaped by how we perceive a situation, not by the stressor itself. If we believe we have the capacity and resources to handle it, we're less likely to experience it as stressful. As the Father of Stress, physiologist Hans Selye, once said, "It is not stress that kills us, it is our reaction to it."

One of the first steps in coping with the bigger stressors in life is shifting how you see them. This isn't easy, but it is possible. Michael Gervais, a world-renowned high-performance psychologist who has coached Olympians, rockstars, and Fortune 100 CEOs, is an expert in helping people navigate stress. He teaches that to change our perception of a situation we need to:

- o   Acknowledge the pain
- o   Recognise that we have options
- o   Trust ourselves.

I'm going to guide you through a few written exercises to help you do just that - so you can begin building your own toolkit for managing life's bigger challenges.

I truly believe we all carry the answers to our problems within us. We're just often too busy to hear them. Let these exercises be a chance to slow down, get quiet, and listen to your own inner wisdom. You may be surprised at what you already know.

Prepare for the exercises

These exercises might feel uncomfortable, emotional, or even pointless. But please give them a try. Often, the more resistance you feel, the more the exercise is needed.

We'll start with timed speed writing. Working under time pressure helps you think more intuitively and stay focused. Too much time allows your logical mind to take over and, if you're already feeling overwhelmed, overthinking can make things worse. So for this exercise, try to set aside rationalising and instead tune in to your intuition.

Take out your journal, get a pen and set a timer for two minutes. Before you begin, take a few deep breaths, sit quietly for a minute and centre yourself in stillness.

When you're ready, work through the following exercises step by step. Don't read ahead until you have completed the step you're on. When doing the writing part of the exercises, write as fast and as much as you can for the full two minutes. Don't stop, even if you think you have nothing more to say. Don't overthink it, just write and see what comes.

Keep your writing. Revisit it in three to six months and you may be pleasantly surprised by how much things have shifted.

ACKNOWLEDGE YOUR PAIN

Get to know your stress

You're going to start by getting to know your main stressor and seeing clearly how it's affecting your life.

Think of the biggest stressor you're currently facing. The one that never sleeps. The one that hums in the background of your mind, quietly but constantly influencing your thoughts, your work, your relationships.

Once you've brought this stressor to mind, set your timer and write about it for two minutes. Go fast, don't overthink. Just let the words flow and explore how it's affecting you. Here are some prompts to guide you:

- What's causing me the most stress?
- How is this stress affecting my life and daily functioning?
- How has it changed my sleep or eating habits?
- How is it impacting my work, relationships, or ability to relax?
- How does it make me feel?

Now that you know your stressor a little better, it's time to look at how you're currently responding to it. Write your answers to the prompts below as quickly as you can.

Set your timer for two minutes and take an honest look at how you're currently coping. Ask yourself:

- What am I currently doing to manage this stressor?
- If I'm trying to cope, why is it still affecting me? What could I do differently?
- If I'm not doing anything about it, why not? What's stopping me from making a change?
- Is something else getting in the way like fatigue, lack of time, money, or support?
- Am I so busy caring for others that I leave no space for myself?
- Deep down, do I feel like I'm not worth the effort?

Whatever your reasons, write them down. This is about understanding, not judging, yourself.

I want you to be deeply honest with yourself now. Even if it makes you feel angry or uncomfortable, take a moment to consider this: is there a reason you might be holding on to your stress?

Sometimes, we believe we work better under pressure. Other times, it's fear. Fear of failure, fear of change, or fear of the unknown. As hard as it is to admit, staying in a state of stress can feel safer than taking action. We might be protecting ourselves from discomfort or uncertainty. As the old saying goes, "Better the devil you know than the devil you don't."

Set a timer for two minutes and reflect: how might staying in this stressful state be helping you in some way?

Here are some questions to guide you:

- In what ways is this stress 'serving' me?
- What do I gain by avoiding change?
- What might happen, both good and bad, if this stressor disappeared?
- What would my life look like without this stress?
- Am I afraid of what change might bring? Why?

By now you hopefully have a clearer sense of what's causing stress in your life and how you've been coping with it. You've acknowledged your pain.

Now it's time to pay attention to how that stress shows up in your body. Maybe it's tight shoulders, a knot in your stomach, or shallow breathing. These signals are your body's way of telling you you're moving into a stress state. When you can spot them early, you give yourself the chance to pause and remember that you have options. Remember, it's not the stress itself that harms us, but how we respond to it.

When we're caught in stress, we often try to think our way out of it. But if the stress feels beyond our control, all that thinking can just make us feel worse. How many times have you spiralled into a black hole, going over and over a problem that feels impossible to solve? Sometimes the best thing we can do is step out of our heads and into a different way of being. As Rabindranath Tagore put it so beautifully: "A mind all logic is like a knife all blade. It makes the hand bleed that uses it."

Stress lives in the body, not just the mind. The following exercises are designed to gently bring you back into your body, where you can begin to feel and release what's really going on beneath the surface.

Have your journal close so that you can make notes as you go. Take your time. Read each exercise slowly and do it before moving on to the next one. This process only works if you give yourself the space to feel, not just think.

Listen to your body

Lie down if you can and close your eyes. Take a deep, slow breath in and as you exhale release all your inner tension with a big sigh.

Repeat four times, making your exhale longer than your inhale. As you breathe out, focus on really letting go. Imagine exhaling every last bit of stale air, creating space for fresh breath to flow in.

When you have finished all four allow your breath to return to normal and simply listen to your breath until you're feeling grounded and at ease.

Then start to slowly scan your body.

Start with your toes. Gently bring your attention to them and notice any sensations you feel. Then slowly move your awareness into your feet, your ankles, shins, calves, knees, and thighs. Keep moving upwards, letting your attention flow gently through your whole body until you reach the very top of your head.

Slowly, gently, peacefully.

If you find your mind wandering, bring your attention back to your breath for a moment and then continue scanning your body.

Once you've finished, take some deep breaths and relax for a while.

How are you feeling? Take a few minutes to write down anything you noticed or felt.

Now, lie down and close your eyes again. Think about what is currently causing you stress.

Picture this stressor clearly in your mind. Let yourself feel it in your body.

What happens to you as you think about it? What emotions come up? Where do you feel them?

Does your breathing change? Does your stomach knot up? Do your jaw or shoulders tighten? Does your head begin to hurt?

There's no need to fix anything, just notice.

Take a moment now to write down how your body responded to your stress and how you're feeling now that you've been focusing on it.

I imagine you're feeling quite different now. Don't worry, the next exercise will leave you feeling good!

KNOW YOU HAVE OPTIONS

Shake it off

You might be feeling a little uncomfortable after that last exercise, so take a few minutes to shake off that heavy energy.

Stand up and move around. Shake out your arms and legs, stretch, bounce, maybe even do a few star jumps. Or splash your face with some cool water to reset.

Keep moving, shaking, jumping, or splashing until you feel the tension release. Then pause, notice how you feel, and enjoy the shift. Hopefully you're feeling lighter, clearer, and maybe even a little refreshed.

The idea behind this series of exercises is to show you something important:

Thinking about your stress triggers real physical reactions

Moving your body or changing your state shifts how you feel within minutes.

I want you to know this: you don't have to feel stressed all the time, even if there are real stressors in your life.

There's a difference between having stressors and feeling stressed. You might not be able to change your financial situation, your boss, or your teenager's moods but you can change what you do in the moment when those worries take over.

When you notice yourself getting caught up in stress, try something simple. Stop thinking and start moving. Get up. Move your body. Change your focus. Know you have options.

Watch your mind

Now that you're more aware of how stress affects your body - and that you have the ability to shift those feelings - let's look at how you can also shift stress mentally.

Instead of focusing all your attention and energy on what's causing you stress, and how out of control you feel, begin to focus on your thoughts. Just notice them. Pay attention to them instead of getting lost in them.

Eckhart Tolle describes this beautifully in *The Power of Now* when he suggests we begin by "watching the thinker". He explains that most of us live with a constant voice in our head and streams of thoughts, inner dialogues, and repetitive patterns that we don't realise we can stop. The key is to step back and simply notice. Instead of being swept away by every thought, begin to listen as an observer. This practice of "watching the thinker" helps create space between you and your thoughts, and with that space comes freedom. Tolle writes:

"Start listening to the voice in your head as often as you can. Pay particular attention to any repetitive thought patterns, those old gramophone records that have been playing in your head perhaps for many years. This is what I mean by 'watching the thinker,' which is another way of saying: listen to the voice in your head, be there as the witnessing presence."

The more you practise "watching the thinker," the more aware you'll become - not just of your thoughts - but of how those thoughts affect your body. You'll start to notice the tension that certain thoughts bring. And it's this awareness that gives you options.

So next time your jaw is clenched or you've got a tension headache, pause and ask yourself "What was I just thinking about?"

Next time you're overwhelmed by your workload, try getting up and going for a walk. Open a window. Take a deep breath. Shift your state. You always have options. You don't have to stay stuck in your stress.

Remember: it's not the empty bank account that harms us, it's the constant anger and shame we feel about it; and it's not the deadline that does the damage, it's the sleepless night spent worrying that leaves us exhausted and vulnerable.

No matter where you are, or what time it is, if you're feeling stressed, know this: you have options.

Shift your focus away from the stressor and turn inward. Notice where the stress is sitting in your body. Where is the tension? The tightness? The heaviness or pain? Notice it, feel it, name it. Then change your state.

TRUST YOURSELF

Something I've noticed in many of my patients who have experienced trauma, is that they don't trust life and they don't trust themselves. This can leave them feeling deeply alone. And this isolation drives them to control everything, perfect everything and keep pushing themselves. It also exhausts them.

When you're stuck in that pattern of trying to control everything and pushing yourself just to keep going, it's easy to lose your rhythm. It's easy to feel out of step with life, disconnected from yourself, and overwhelmed by everything around you. It can feel like you're drowning.

And when you feel like you're drowning, trusting in yourself and your own abilities can feel almost impossible.

If the words "trust in yourself" don't resonate with you right now that's okay. Self-trust isn't something you either have or don't have – it's something you build. You build it slowly through setting goals and following through on them.

Because this book is about health and energy, a good place to begin is by setting small, achievable health goals. Each one you meet will not only help you build trust in yourself, it will also begin to lay the foundation for better health and more energy.

These foundations for good health are often called the four pillars of health. Think of the pillars or columns in a building - they're there to provide strength and support. If the pillars are strong, the structure can withstand wind and storms.

It's the same with your health. When you're eating well, moving your body, getting good sleep, and taking time to rest, you'll feel steadier and more supported even when life is stressful. But when those pillars are weak, when you're not eating or sleeping well, not moving, and not making time to unwind, everything feels harder, and it's easy to fall apart.

In the next chapter, I'll share simple ways to strengthen these four pillars. But go gently. Just pick one or two ideas to start with and practise them each day until they become a habit. When they feel steady, come back and add another.

11, THE PILLARS OF HEALTH

PILLAR I: EAT WELL

If you've been following the guidelines in Part 1, you're now hopefully eating in a way that supports your body - balancing your blood sugars, lowering inflammation, healing your gut, and feeding your microbiome. That foundation is essential. But when life becomes particularly stressful, your body often needs a little extra support. Two key things to keep in mind are cutting back on stimulants such as caffeine and alcohol, and making sure you're getting enough of the stress-supporting vitamins B, C, and D.

Let's start with stimulants. I'll be honest, I love coffee and drink it every day. In fact, I'm sipping on one right now! But it's important to understand its downsides so you can make an informed choice about what's right for you.

Caffeine gives you a quick lift because it stimulates the release of adrenaline and noradrenaline. The problem is, this also pushes your body into 'fight or flight' mode, which can leave you feeling restless, anxious, or jittery. Over time, too much caffeine can raise cortisol or disrupt its natural rhythm, making it harder for your body to recover from stress. It also blocks the signals that help you feel sleepy, disrupting your natural sleep cycle.

If you're dealing with insomnia, afternoon crashes, jitteriness, or heart palpitations, these may be your body's way of telling you that you're overdoing the caffeine. As a general guide, one or two cups of coffee in the morning is enough. Also be mindful that caffeine is in tea, chocolate, energy drinks, many soft drinks and some over-the-counter medicines such as pain killers, cold/flu medications and some weight-loss products.

Alcohol is another stimulant that can be especially hard on the body during stressful times. While it may feel relaxing at first, alcohol actually places more strain on your adrenal glands. It raises cortisol levels, disrupts blood sugar balance, and interferes with deep, restorative sleep. Over time, it also depletes important nutrients like vitamins B and C. If you're struggling with stress or fatigue, it helps to keep alcohol to a minimum. And when you do drink, always have it with food rather than on an empty stomach.

Now let's turn to the nutrients that help your body cope with stress. B vitamins play a central role in supporting your nervous system, but stress burns through them quickly. Because they're water-soluble, your body doesn't store them so you need a steady supply every day. Animal products such as meat, dairy, and eggs are rich sources. If you're vegan, focus on fortified nutritional yeast, mushrooms, avocados, sunflower seeds, and legumes. For a deeper look at the B vitamins, revisit Chapter 2.

Vitamin C is equally important. It's essential for producing your stress hormones, and your adrenal glands actually store some of the highest concentrations of vitamin C in your body. It also plays a crucial role in immunity. During stressful times, your need for vitamin C increases, so include plenty of citrus fruits, strawberries, leafy greens, and other vitamin C-rich foods in your diet.

Vitamin D is just as vital. It supports hormone balance, strengthens the immune system, and helps regulate mood. These are all disrupted by ongoing stress. Many people are low in vitamin D without realising it, so try to spend some time in the sun each day and add vitamin D-rich foods such as oily fish and eggs to your diet.

PILLAR 2: EXERCISE REGULARLY

Getting outdoors in nature and sunshine every day is key to reducing stress and recovering a sense of perspective on life. Regular movement also improves your cells' sensitivity to insulin, which plays an important role in keeping your blood sugar levels steady.

However, be aware that when you're dealing with deep fatigue, too much exercise can leave you feeling worse - sore, drained, and heavy. This is called post-exertional malaise. So choose gentle movement that feels good: a slow walk, a swim in the sea, yin or restorative yoga, playing with your kids, or pottering in your garden. Aim for activities that move your body without depleting it and try to exercise outdoors so that you get some vitamin D.

PILLAR 3: MAKE TIME TO RELAX

"I didn't get there by wishing for it or hoping for it, but by working for it."
- Estée Lauder

As contradictory as it might sound, relaxing takes effort. Simply wishing things felt different, or hoping stress will disappear on its own, rarely changes much. To truly relax, you need to take action - and not just once in a while. A bit of downtime on holiday won't sustain you. Relaxation has to become part of your everyday life, woven into your daily routine.

Here are a few simple tools you can use to help yourself relax. Try them out and see what feels right for you. Once you find something that makes a difference, try to make space for it every single day. And yes, I really do mean every single day! What we practise in calm moments is what strengthens us when stress shows up.

Create your own routine

This is my personal favourite "action" for relaxing. When I went back to university as a mature student with two young children, life was full. Between studying, parenting, and keeping the house running, there was no time for myself, let alone time to relax.

So, I began setting my alarm a little earlier. Instead of leaping out of bed and rushing into the day, I'd make a cup of coffee, climb back into bed, and read a book. That simple routine became one of the best things I ever did for myself. And many years later, I still start my mornings the same way. No matter how busy my day ahead, I always begin with coffee and a book. Every day, without fail, I have that moment of calm just for me, doing something I love.

What routine can you create for yourself? What moment of calm can you squeeze into your day – every day?

Journal, "brain-dump", or write lists

Many people find that writing each day helps them get perspective on their lives. Some journal for clarity, others jot down their worries or to-do lists before bed to clear their minds. A patient of mine told me she hates to write so does mind-maps instead.

Daily writing doesn't have to take long but done regularly it creates surprising ease and calm.

Do something creative

You don't need to be an artist to create. You don't even need to share what you create. All you need to do is have some fun. Write, draw, paint, garden, cook, do some woodwork, make some jewellery – anything to free your mind and nourish your soul.

Create some quiet time

If the idea of meditation feels off-putting, try thinking of it simply as quiet time. You don't need to sit cross-legged for an hour. Just find ten minutes to sit quietly, breathe, and listen to the world around you.

A friend once told me how, with five young kids at home, her daily ritual was to "go park the car." She'd slip away and sit alone in the car for ten minutes of blissful peace. That was her meditation and it worked.

Breathe deeply

If you've only got five minutes a day, spend it breathing. Deep breathing is simple, powerful, and can be done anywhere. Even just two minutes a day can begin to calm your nervous system.

This beautiful technique comes from Rudolph Ballentine's *Radical Healing*:

"Lying on your back in a relaxed position, inhale from the toes up to the top of the head. Then follow with your attention from the crown to the feet as you exhale. Don't force the breath, it should be relaxed and gentle – it's the energy flow that you want to allow to maximise – not the muscular exertion of the chest. Imagine that as you exhale you are throwing out all your troubling thoughts and feelings. As you inhale you are taking in light, clarity and serenity."

I really encourage you to find something small, simple and achievable. Something you can do every day to rest and relax. We often over-complicate the idea of relaxing, when all we really need to do is take a few minutes to be alone, to slow down and to breathe.

PILLAR 4: PRIORITISE SLEEP

Your sleep is shaped by what you do during the day, especially how you care for your body, your energy, and your routine. When you're eating well, moving regularly, and creating moments of calm, sleep often improves naturally.

Your internal body clock, known as your circadian rhythm, is what keeps your body in tune with the natural cycle of day and night. It's controlled by a tiny area in your brain that responds to light coming through your eyes. When it's bright outside, your body clock tells you to be alert and awake. As evening comes and light fades, your body begins to release melatonin, a hormone that makes you feel sleepy and helps prepare you for rest. This rhythm affects not just your sleep, but also your energy, mood, and even how your body digests food. Unfortunately, your body clock is easily disrupted by irregular sleep patterns, shift work and artificial light. A consistent bed-time routine coupled with getting natural light in your eyes during the day and keeping evenings darker helps keep this clock running smoothly.

Many people who struggle to sleep have poor sleep hygiene. Sleep hygiene is the term used for the everyday habits and routines that set you up for a good night's rest. Just like brushing your teeth helps protect your dental health, simple practices around bedtime help protect your sleep. Good sleep hygiene supports the natural rhythms of your body, making it easier to fall asleep, stay asleep, and wake feeling refreshed.

Here are some simple ways to improve your sleep hygiene:

- **Go to sleep at the same time** every night.
- **Wake up at the same time** every day, no matter how well (or poorly) you slept.
- **Get sunlight or bright light in your eyes** as soon as you wake. This will suppress melatonin and help you feel more awake and alert.
- **Exercise in the mornings,** not the evenings. During exercise your heart rate, body temperature and stress hormones all rise and can delay the natural evening rise of melatonin. Bright lights in gyms or exercise spaces also add to the problem by telling your brain it's still daytime.

o **Create a calming bedtime routine.** Just as your morning routine helps you wake up, evening rituals prepare your body to wind down. Doing the same thing each night sends a gentle signal that it's time to rest. For many people, a warm bath, reading a book, or another simple ritual helps the mind slow down and switch off.

o **Limit screen time before bed.** Blue light from phones, TVs, and computers can block the evening rise of melatonin, the hormone that helps you feel sleepy. Try to switch off devices at least two hours before bedtime so your body knows it's time to unwind.

o **Some medications can interfere with sleep.** If you've been prescribed any of the following and are finding it hard to rest, talk to your doctor about finding an alternative:
  o SSRI antidepressants
  o Corticosteroids
  o Beta blockers
  o Pseudoephedrine (found in many cold and flu remedies).

o **Watch out for hidden caffeine.** Caffeine is not just in coffee - it's also in chocolate, energy drinks, some painkillers, and even cold and flu medications.

If better sleep hygiene isn't enough on its own, turn to the remedies at the back of this book. The herbal and homoeopathic options there may help you find deeper, more restful sleep.

PART 3. TURN TO YOUR SOUL

At the beginning of this book, I mentioned that healing is not about fixing or changing yourself. It's about learning to accept yourself just as you are - wounds, scars, and all.

In the next few chapters, you'll find suggestions and exercises that invite healing on a very deep level. Some of these may stir up painful memories or feelings, so I encourage you to move through them with care.

If you've been through trauma, consider finding a counsellor who can walk alongside you on this part of your journey. You don't have to do it alone. If an exercise feels overwhelming or brings up a lot of emotion, give yourself a couple of weeks before trying another one. Healing takes time, and it's okay to go slowly.

And if you're not yet feeling strong or energised, it may be best to pause here. Put the book down for a few months and return once you've worked through the guidance in Parts 1 and 2. Trust that there is no rush. Healing unfolds at the pace that's right for you.

12, The Weight You've Been Carrying

"Visualize an iceberg, which is only about 10 percent above water and 90 percent underwater. Most of our behaviour and decisions are driven by what is below the water, what we cannot see."
– Christine Hassler

A close friend of mine has lived with severe fatigue for years. I remember opening her pantry one day and being blown away by how immaculate it was. Every jar labelled, every item decanted and arranged in perfect order. I teased her about it but wondered how she had time to do all that. She was a single mum working full time.

I also wondered why she did it. The perfection, the organization - all of it felt like the tip of the iceberg. What was beneath?

When patients first come to me, they often talk about their fatigue as controlling their lives. Their lack of energy dictates what they can do, who they can see, even what they eat. They speak about being passed from doctor to doctor, test to test, without real answers. It's no wonder they feel lost and out of control.

But when we gently explore their past, a different pattern emerges. Not a lack of control. Too much control.

Often, they've burned themselves out by trying to hold everything together. They've spent years over-controlling their environment, their

128

schedules, even themselves. Many are high achievers: A-students, top of their class, neat, reliable, driven.

Many of them also know everything about health. They're experts on biochemistry, gut healing, nervous system regulation. Yet they can't remember the last time they truly let themselves rest.

How have you coped with what life has thrown at you? What strategies or coping mechanisms have you developed over the years? What does the tip of your iceberg look like?

Do you keep yourself constantly busy - cleaning, organising, helping, working - because the stillness feels too uncomfortable? Do you distract yourself with health research, trying to control your symptoms by learning everything you can about nutrition, protocols, or supplements? Do you push yourself to eat perfectly, move perfectly, live perfectly, yet never really let yourself rest?

If this sounds familiar, just start noticing it. Ask yourself: What am I really trying to control? And what would it feel like, just as an experiment, to let go, even a little?

ARE YOU STUCK IN A STRESS RESPONSE?

When Susie first walked into my office, she looked the picture of health. She was in her early fifties, elegant, fit, and seemingly full of energy. She followed a strict diet free of meat, gluten, dairy, and sugar, and packed with vegetables. Yet she had come to see me because she was exhausted. She'd been living with fatigue and fibromyalgia since her early twenties and now menopause was hitting hard - insomnia, food intolerances, perfume sensitivities, irritable bowel syndrome, and constant infections.

It's something I see so often. Real *dis-ease*. A controlled exterior coupled with so much internal chaos.

Once Susie opened up, I could clearly see where the chaos was rooted. Her father had been a deeply unstable alcoholic and, as the eldest child, she had spent her childhood protecting her siblings. Although she'd left home nearly 30 years ago, her body was still trapped in a stress response. Still in fight-or-flight.

The Dunedin Study has tracked 1,037 people from birth and is now in its fifth decade, with over 1,300 publications on health, development, and behaviour. One key finding is that children exposed to violence or early adversity are nearly twice as likely to show raised levels of inflammation compared to those not maltreated. Sadly, as developmental researchers Moffitt and Grawe observed, "violence exposure is one of the most common and severe sources of human stress."

I see this reflected time and again in my patients with fatigue or burnout - many have been exposed to violence or trauma in childhood or early adulthood. While they often feel they've processed it through counselling or psychological support, their bodies are still, for some reason, stuck in that highly responsive, survival mode they relied on as children.

I personally didn't realise I was stuck in a state of 'hyper-alertness' because it was the only state I'd ever known. It felt normal to me. In my thirties, I struggled with a tight neck and shoulders, heart palpitations, breathlessness, and insomnia even though I had a wonderful husband, two beautiful daughters, and a job I loved. One day, my chiropractor stopped mid-treatment and asked, "What are you holding onto, Ruth? You are so rigid it's as if someone has poured concrete into your body." I was taken aback. I didn't think I was stressed - but clearly, my body was.

IT'S OKAY. YOU'RE HERE NOW

If you grew up in a home with violence, addiction, trauma, or instability - where, as a child, you had no control over what was happening - there's a good chance you developed ways to create a sense of control later in life.

And that's okay. That sense of control helped you get through what you had to get through.

But stop for a minute and look at where you are now. Are you living somewhere stable and safe? Do you have people in your life who love you? Who care for you? I'm hoping you can answer yes. If you can say yes, then take a moment to remind yourself that you are right here, right now and everything is okay.

You're no longer that child feeling helpless as your parents fight, you're no longer that young girl who was powerless to say 'no'. You're an adult now. You're your own person now.

You're in a different time and a different place. You're safe. You no longer need to stay trapped in a constant fight-or-flight response. Try saying these words out loud:

I'm right here, right now. I'm safe. I'm strong. I'm supported.

All is well in my world.

Write them on a couple of sticky notes and stick them where you'll see them often, for example, your mirror, toilet door, fridge door, back of your phone or computer screen. Every time you see the words, take a deep breath in and out, slow yourself down and allow the words to really sink in and reassure you that you're safe now.

If an affirmation doesn't feel right to you, then consider finding an "anchor". An anchor can be anything that brings you back to your present moment and reminds you where you are now and that you're safe.

Some people wear bands around their wrists, some people buy themselves a special piece of jewellery like a watch or a ring, some people get tattoos. Whatever you choose, let it be a constant reminder that you're no longer in that situation where you felt small and powerless and there was nothing you could do. You're in a safe space now. You can let go.

YOU CAN REWRITE YOUR STORY

Letting go of old stories takes time and, unfortunately, needs to be done again and again and again. It's like dirty laundry…you think you've emptied the washing basket and the next morning it's full again!

In order to be able to rewrite your story, you need to start by writing your story as you know it so far. Start by writing about your childhood - where you came from, who your parents were, and what you've lived through. I mentioned this earlier in the book, and if you haven't done it yet, I encourage you to do it now. You need to know your own life story. You need to understand what weight you're carrying, or what boulder you're still pushing uphill. As Brené Brown says, "Only when we're brave enough to explore the darkness will we discover the infinite power of our light."

One of the hardest stories to let go of is the belief that you're weak or powerless. It's a story I see so many people with fatigue carrying. If this feeling comes from a past traumatic experience, I gently encourage you to seek support from a professional counsellor or therapist. You don't have to carry it all alone, and life doesn't always have to feel like a battle. Working with someone skilled in trauma can make a profound difference.

BEAUTIFUL PEOPLE DO NOT JUST HAPPEN

The story I'm about to share is a difficult one. It involves a traumatic experience, but also incredible survival and strength. I'm including it not to shock or unsettle you, but because I believe stories like this remind us of what the human spirit is capable of. If you're feeling fragile today, you might want to pause and return to it another time. Please read it only if you feel grounded and ready.

While at university in South Africa, I volunteered at a Rape Crisis, helping get survivors of rape to safety and accompanying them to hospitals, police stations and court. The story of rape-survivor Alison Botha helped many survivors cope with what they were going through.

In December 1994 Alison was abducted by two men, raped, stabbed and left for dead. Somehow, she survived this monstrous moment in her life and went on to help thousands of other survivors through her talks and books.

She always said that although we can't control what happens in life, we can choose how we respond to it.

A film entitled Alison was later made about her. After seeing it, she said: "I think they have captured the essence of it – the horror and the fear and then that complete miraculous lightness of: 'Oh wow, how did I survive this?'"

I'm sharing her story because no matter what you've been through - no matter how monstrous, awful, or painful - you're still here.

You are a survivor.

Look back and see, as Alison saw, that complete miraculous lightness of survival.

It's hard to look back and see where you've come from. It's even harder to acknowledge what you've been through and to accept that it has shaped who you are. But if you want to move forward and shift out of your continual stress response, you need to accept your scars as part of you.

I love how Elisabeth Kubler-Ross says beautiful people do not just happen:

"The most beautiful people we have known are those who have known defeat, known suffering, known struggle, known loss, and have found their way out of the depths. These persons have an appreciation, a sensitivity, and an understanding of

life that fills them with compassion, gentleness, and a deep loving concern. Beautiful people do not just happen."

Think of a bonsai tree and how it grows. It starts with the potential to be a huge, powerful tree, but it's kept trapped in a space far too small for it and its growth and development are constricted for many years. Yet these very circumstances that hold it back, enable it to become a rare, magical beauty.

It's the same with diamonds – they're only formed under intense pressure and heat.

And it's the same with you. What constrictions, what pressures, what circumstances have created you? Remember, beautiful people do not just happen.

THE HARDEST LETTER YOU MAY EVER WRITE

If you recognise you're caught in a stress response, this exercise may help you gently shift out of it. But before you begin, take a moment to ask yourself if you feel safe enough to let go. Your stress response is here to protect you, so there's no need to push or hurry your healing. What matters most is that you feel safe and secure.

If you do feel ready, then try this exercise.

And don't worry - you're going to explore the *impact* your trauma had on you, not the trauma itself. You won't need to go over any details of what happened in your past and you won't need to relive anything. Instead, you'll be focusing on honouring how far you've come. The essence of this exercise is to recognise the strength it took to survive, and the ways you've grown because of it.

Before we begin, I want to invite you into a quiet, safe space. This is a deeply personal exercise and it may bring up a lot of painful emotions. Read through it first and if it feels too much to do alone then find a counsellor to support you through it.

When you're ready, sit quietly and bring to mind an event, circumstance, or person in your life that hurt you. Something that changed you. Perhaps something you believe damaged you or threw you off course.

Now, write a *thank you* letter to that event or person. Yes – I said "thank you letter". Thank the experience for shaping you, in whatever way it did. And thank yourself for your inner strength, for getting through it, and for becoming the person you are today.

I know this can feel confronting, especially if it touches on things you've tried hard to forget. So don't rush. Go slowly. Be kind to yourself. Focus on what carried you through. Focus on the parts of you that are still here. Your inner strength and resilience.

Many of us stay stuck in survival mode for years after something painful happens. This is a chance to gently begin letting go. To soften the grip that old pain might still have on your body and nervous system. It's a small but powerful step toward healing.

13, START LETTING GO

Feeling safe and stepping out of your stress response is essential to healing. So is understanding the beliefs that have shaped how you see yourself, your life, and your worth. Many of these beliefs may not even be yours to begin with.

Genes are the tiny units of inheritance that guide how our bodies are built and function. For years, it was believed they determined everything. But science now shows that genes can be switched on or off depending on lifestyle and environment. This field is called epigenetics and it's taught us that even though we carry our genes, we also have some power over how they're expressed.

Beliefs work the same way. We inherit patterns of thinking passed down through generations. They may once have helped our families survive, but that doesn't mean they're true or that we must keep living by them.

Philosopher Bertrand Russell once said, "I would never die for my beliefs because I might be wrong." If a man devoted to logic and truth could question his own beliefs, perhaps we should too.

Not every story we carry is ours, or even true. Just as we can shape how our genes are expressed through lifestyle, we can also choose which beliefs to keep and which to release. We don't have to settle for what we've inherited.

Here is a speed writing exercise to encourage you explore your personal beliefs and values. Write on one topic at a time, giving yourself sixty seconds on each of the following:

- o **Money** – What does money mean to me? What comes to mind when I hear the word? Does it spark joy or stress? Is it important to me? What childhood memories or feelings come up?
- o **Work** – What does work mean to me? How do I feel when I hear the word? Do I work hard and, if so, for what reason?
- o **Family** – What does family mean to me? What is my role in my family? How do I feel about this role? What are my responsibilities, and how do I carry them?
- o **Gender** – What gender do I identify with? What does that mean to me? How has my gender shaped my life, my work, my role in the family, and my place in society?

Once you've completed the topics above, take a moment to reflect:

- o Whose beliefs and values are these?
- o Where did they come from?
- o Have you intentionally chosen them, or simply absorbed and inherited them from others?
- o Do they support you and help you grow or are they holding you back?

Mark Manson wrote, "The values we pick up throughout our lives crystallise and form a sediment on top of our personality".

What sediment is on top of your personality? And is it time to clear some of it away?

MAKING SPACE

"Make space for what you love. Clutter obscures what's most important."
- Marie Kondo

This might sound a little odd, but with many of my patients who are struggling with fatigue, we often end up talking about decluttering their homes. So many of them sit in my therapy room and tell me how overwhelmed they feel by the mess, how they can't bring themselves to throw things away, how they wish they had more storage space.

These are the same patients who find it hard to let go of long-held emotions, thought patterns, or beliefs.

Think of your home. If you never emptied the bins or flushed the toilet, things would quickly get unpleasant. Your body works the same way. If it holds on to all its waste - its toxins and rubbish – you will get very sick.

And it's the same with your mind and emotions. If you hold on to old thoughts, beliefs, or emotions, they start clogging your mental and emotional space, leaving you tired, flat, and weighed down. Just like your bins won't empty themselves, your emotional clutter won't clear on its own. If you're dealing with fatigue, learning to let go, intentionally and regularly, is a powerful step towards energy.

And you can start today. Begin with something small like your wallet or handbag. Throw out the rubbish, receipts or anything you don't use regularly. Then choose a drawer or cupboard. Take everything out. Clean the space. Only put back what you love, use, and truly want to keep. After that move onto something bigger.

It sounds straightforward, but don't be surprised if it's harder than you expect. You'll likely come across things that were expensive, given as gifts, or once held meaning. Letting go can feel uncomfortable but try to do it anyway. Thank the item for what it brought to your life, say goodbye, and let it go. Only keep what you love and use now. Only keep what truly serves you now.

MINDING YOUR ENERGY

Once you've decluttered your home, you will find your energy starts to shift and you'll feel more comfortable doing the next few exercises which will help you make space for more energy to come into your life.

Take a moment to think about your to-do list, your diary, and all the responsibilities you're juggling. Then ask yourself honestly: *Do I have the time or space in my life for more energy?*

We often blame ourselves for feeling exhausted or unproductive. But maybe the problem isn't that we're not doing enough. Maybe it's that we're doing too much, trying to be too much, and carrying far more than we need to.

Try this exercise now. It's similar to decluttering your home but this time it's decluttering your diary.

Step 1: Write it all down

Grab a blank piece of paper and write down everything you're doing day-to-day, including:

- o   Your work
- o   Each work project or responsibility
- o   Family and home commitments
- o   Volunteering or community roles
- o   Regular routines like cooking, errands, school drop-offs, etcetera.

Step 2: How do you feel about each thing?

Next to each activity, write down how you feel about it:

- o **Love** – it lights you up or feels meaningful
- o **Hate** – you dread it, or it leaves you feeling flat or resentful
- o **50/50** – you don't mind it, but it doesn't energise you either.

Be honest, this is just for you.

Step 3: Sort it into columns

Take a new piece of paper and divide it into six columns. Label them:

1. **Love** - Things I love doing and want to keep doing
2. **Reframe** - Things I need to do but could reframe or see differently
3. **Delegate** - Things I need to do but could delegate or ask for help with
4. **Stop now** - Things I hate doing and can stop now
5. **Stop in 3 months** - Things I hate doing and will stop in 3 months
6. **Stop in 6-12 months** - Things I hate doing and will stop in 6–12 months

Then go back to your original list and begin placing each activity in the column that fits best.

Start with your Love items. They go straight into the Love column. These are your energy givers.

For Hate items, ask yourself:

- o Can I stop this now? → *Column 4*
- o Can I plan to let it go in a few months? → *Column 5*
- o Will it take longer, but I know I'll get there? → *Column 6*
- o Could I ask someone to help with this? → *Column 3*

For 50/50s, check in:

- o Could this feel lighter if I changed how I think about it? → *Column 2*
- o Could someone else help with it? → *Column 3*
- o Or is it quietly draining more than I realised? → *Reconsider where it belongs.*

Why this matters

The first time I did this exercise I had a huge to-do list. When I wrote it all down I got a bit of a fright. Once I'd sorted everything into Love, Hate, and 50/50, I realised there were only *three* things in my Love column.

I was spending most of my time doing things I didn't want to do. No wonder I felt so exhausted.

At the time, I was also stuck in a job I really didn't like but was locked into a year-long contract. I couldn't leave yet but writing it in Column 6 helped. It reminded me it *would* end eventually. That small shift gave me more breathing space. It helped me feel like I wasn't completely stuck.

This exercise might seem simple, but it can be powerful. It gives you a starting point, a way to see your life more clearly and a sense of where you want to head. Keep this piece of paper somewhere visible. Let it remind you of what matters, what lifts you up, and what you're ready to let go of.

LET LIFE SUPPORT YOU

When I was preparing to write this book, I didn't want to include the words my patients had shared with me in confidence. So instead, I interviewed people who were experiencing burnout but were not under

141

my care. It was a fascinating and moving process. Two emotions that came up again and again were shame and guilt. Here's what some of them shared:

"I feel guilty, I'm not participating on the level of life I want to."

"I never feel present with my family. It's like I'm watching a movie."

"I feel useless. I'm not contributing anything."

"I feel guilty. I don't have the energy to communicate. I don't have enthusiasm for anything."

"I feel like I'm faking my existence."

"I'm a very good mother and wife but I'm not satisfied. I'm not fulfilling myself. I wake up and don't feel excited for the day."

"I'm the handbrake in our family."

Their words made me reflect on how lonely the journey through fatigue can be and how many people silently struggle without ever asking for help.

Do you remember learning about the Law of Conservation of Energy at school: that energy is neither created nor destroyed, it's only converted from one form into another?

Take a moment to sit with that. Maybe even write about it in your journal.

Ask yourself:

- o Do I allow energy to flow in my life?
- o Do I let in as much as I give out? Or am I constantly giving without ever receiving?
- o Do I help everyone else but find it hard to ask for, or accept, help myself?

Restoring your energy means letting it flow both ways, receiving as well as giving. As Alexander McCall Smith said, "We think that we have to learn how to give, but we forget about accepting things, which can be much harder than giving...Accepting another person's gift is allowing him to express his feelings for you."

I've lived in quite a few different countries now, so I know how hard it is to leave your home and start over. I think that's why I often attract patients who are immigrants and I see in them a deep, quiet tiredness that I know so well. That tiredness that comes from feeling alone and unsupported.

I see this same kind of fatigue in people who grew up with an absent parent, or a parent who was physically present but emotionally unavailable.

You may not be able to replace the home or support you've lost, but you can begin to let life support you in new ways. You can learn to receive energy in different forms and allow it to flow again.

The Harvard Study of Adult Development is an ongoing research project that has followed the lives of a group of men since 1938, tracking their development and ageing. One of the original goals was to understand what predicts healthy ageing. Over more than 80 years, participants have undergone regular medical exams, interviews, and psychological assessments.

The most interesting conclusion has been drawn - at midlife it's not a person's cholesterol levels or other biomarkers that predict longevity, it is in fact whether or not they are satisfied in their relationships.

What this shows is simple but profound: caring relationships and supportive communities aren't just nice to have – they're essential to health and wellbeing. Try reaching out, building connections and allowing yourself to lean on others. Friendship and a sense of belonging are integral to healing.

In addition to building relationships within your community, you can also look to nature for support.

One of my patients, who lived through childhood trauma, discovered that swimming in the ocean gives her a deep sense of renewal and peace. She now swims every morning as part of her routine.

In my own life, I've found that walking in nature reminds me I'm part of something bigger - that I belong, and I'm never truly alone, no matter where in the world I am. So I try to go for a walk in nature every day.

What supports you in life and how can you make this support part of your normal, daily routine?

EXPLORE YOUR BOUNDARIES

Whilst we're talking about energy and how it flows, I want to draw your attention to how our physical bodies mirror our energetic selves.

For example, if you're struggling with leaky gut, take a look at your personal boundaries – are you absorbing things that you shouldn't be? Are you taking on other people's energy?

Similarly, if you're dealing with chronic inflammation, is your body on constant alert? What small things are slipping into your energy field and quietly irritating or inflaming you?

Start thinking of your energy as something separate from yourself - something that needs to be nourished, nurtured, and protected. Imagine it as a precious golden liquid that you carry around in a bucket. But the bucket isn't very strong, and that energy can leak out through all sorts of little holes.

Take a moment now with a pen and paper and look at the boundaries you've set in different areas of your life. As you reflect, ask yourself: Are these boundaries truly protecting and supporting my energy or are they allowing my energy to leak out?

If you haven't put boundaries in place, gently ask yourself why not. What are you afraid might happen if you did?

Ask yourself these questions:

- o **Work** – How much do I allow my work, studies, or other projects to encroach on - or 'leak into' - my personal and family time? Is my work life clearly separated from my home life, or do I let the two blur together? Do I stick to set work or study hours? Do I only respond to emails, texts, or calls during those times? Do I take lunch breaks?
- o **Family** – What do I do, away from my family, to maintain my own sense of identity? How and when do I step out of the roles I play - as a parent, child, or sibling - and make space to feed my soul, have fun, and just be me?
- o **Finances** – Am I spending a lot of my energy worrying about money? If so, what small structures could I put in place to help me feel more secure? Who could I reach out to for support or advice?
- o **Volunteering** – Am I the friend or family member everyone relies on because I never say no? The colleague who helps everyone with their presentations or reports? Am I the mum always putting her hand up at school functions? How much time do I spend giving to others compared to looking after myself or simply resting?
- o **Perfectionism** – I'm including this because you might be someone who needs to set some gentle boundaries around your own expectations. Do you end up doing all the cleaning because your teenagers don't do it "well enough"? Do you often think it's just easier to do things yourself because no one else will do them the way you would?

If you're feeling tired and stretched thin, it may be time to loosen your expectations. Let some things be "good enough." And if you struggle with boundaries, here's a gentle challenge: for one week, say "no" to people and projects, even if it feels selfish. Use that time to rest or do something fun just for you.

Remember, "no" is a complete sentence. You don't need to explain or justify it. If you're tired, lie on the couch. Just say no and relax.

You might have strong personal boundaries and feel confident that your energy isn't leaking out, yet you're still exhausted. If that's the case, it may be time to look at what you're absorbing from your environment.

Think of a museum curator. They carefully choose what belongs in the space and care for it with intention. Are you doing the same in your own life? Are you choosing who and what you allow in? Are you choosing the news you listen to and the social media you scroll through?

Everything around you either nourishes your energy or drains it. And you get to choose. You are the curator of your own energy.

14, Keep Letting Go

Wow! You've made it to the final chapter of this book - well done. I hope by now your energy has begun to shift and that you're nourishing both your body and yourself. I also hope you've been able to let go of a few things, creating space for energy to flow more freely in your life. Hopefully you've started decluttering your home and your to-do list, reconsidering beliefs that were never really yours, and strengthening your boundaries. Quite a lot of work, isn't it!

Now, in this last chapter, we'll return to your physical body and listen to what it's trying to tell you one last time. The next exercise can feel a little unusual at first but stay with it. You might be surprised by what your body wants you to hear.

The table below contains five different groups of symptoms. Go through each group and circle or mark any symptoms you regularly experience.

After marking the symptoms you experience, add up how many symptoms you've marked in each group and write the total in the space provided. Then compare the totals to see which groups carry the most weight. For example, if you have 5/6 symptoms in Group D and 7/17 in E, then D carries the most weight because you have most of the symptoms listed there. I hope this makes sense?

Please do this before moving on with the rest of this chapter.

A	B
Hormonal/period problems	
Constipation	Bags under your eyes
Bloating	Skin lacks elasticity
Abdominal pain/cramps	Discolouration of skin
Fatigue	Fluid retention
Tired eyes	Frequent urination
Low libido	Poor circulation
Headaches or a heavy head	Lower back ache
Poor digestion	Fatigue
Flatulence/gas	Low libido
Body odour	Dark urine
Itchy skin	Bad breath
Skin rashes	
Total A: ____/13	**Total B: ____/11**

C	D
Frequent chest infections	Pimples, acne
Difficulty breathing	Rashes
Tight chest	Itching skin
"Weak" lungs	Eczema/dermatitis
Poor circulation	Psoriasis
Fatigue	Mouth ulcers
Pale skin	
Total C: ____/7	**Total D: ____/6**

E	
Constipation	Postnasal drip
Diarrhoea	Sinusitis
Bloating	Pimples or acne
Gas/flatulence	Rashes, itching skin
Abdominal cramps	Eczema
Bad breath	Recurring tonsillitis
Body odour	Liver or gallbladder issues
Snotty nose	Respiratory problems
Blocked nose	
Total E: ____/17	

You'll probably find most of your symptoms fall into two or three groups. Each group relates to one of the main organs of elimination as follows:

A: Liver

B: Kidneys

C: Lungs

D: Skin

E: Large intestine/colon.

These five organs work together to clear waste and toxins from your body. If one is under strain, the others often have to "pick up the slack," which is why it's common to find more than one out of balance at the same time.

Over the next few pages, I'll walk you through simple, gentle ways to support these organs so they function more effectively and your symptoms ease. However, before doing so I want to be clear that this is not a detox protocol.

There are many different detox programs out there, and while I'm not opposed to them in general, I don't recommend strict detoxing if you're living with deep fatigue. When your body is exhausted and energy reserves are already low, harsh detox approaches can do more harm than good. They may bring short-term relief, but for someone who is depleted, they often lead to a crash - sometimes worse than before. That's why a softer, more supportive approach is needed when your body is running on empty.

My approach to supporting your organs of elimination is gentle, and with each organ I'll also talk about a specific emotion. This is because a shift in focus is needed - a shift away from trying to "fix" your body and towards listening to what it's trying to tell you.

Your physical symptoms are not random; they're messages from your body, and it's vital to listen to them. It's easy to become caught up in diets, exercise routines, therapies, or pills and believe that's enough. While these may bring some relief, true healing goes deeper. It requires paying attention to the emotional layers as well.

I've offered a few ways to begin that journey but please remember this is just the start. Healing your emotions takes time and it's something you don't have to do alone. Find the right support. Some things are too heavy to carry on your own.

A note on resistance...

It's completely normal to feel resistance as you start learning more about yourself.

As you read through this chapter, you might notice your symptoms pointing clearly to one or two organs and then feel sceptical when you read the emotions associated with them. You might even think, "This is a load of nonsense!"

That's okay. Go with it anyway. Let the ideas sit with you. Let them roll around in your mind for a while.

Try journaling about those emotions. What do they mean to you? How have they shown up in your life? Or how haven't they? Go for a long walk and gently ask yourself why your body might be sending you these messages.

Sometimes, these emotions are ones we've completely pushed down and suppressed so we don't think they are a problem. Let this be a gentle invitation to bring them to light.

A, YOUR LIVER

Your liver is the second-largest organ in your body. It filters blood from your digestive system before it reaches your heart, ensuring it's clean and safe. It also metabolises carbohydrates, fats, and proteins, regulates blood sugar, stores nutrients, activates vitamin D, produces cholesterol, and makes bile. Basically, your liver is essential to your health!

If you're noticing symptoms from Column A, it doesn't indicate liver disease but it may suggest your liver is working a bit harder than it should and could benefit from some support.

If your liver isn't functioning optimally, you'll likely experience many of the symptoms listed above - along with issues related to your large intestine and skin. This is a sign to start paying close attention to the quality of what you're putting into and onto your body.

Remember, your liver filters and cleans your blood so anything you eat, drink or even put onto your skin, needs to be processed by your liver. In our modern world where we're surrounded by additives and preservatives in almost everything, our liver can easily become overworked.

Take a moment to count how many products you've used on your skin and hair today. If you're a woman, it's probably somewhere between 10 and 15. Now consider that each of those products can contain another 10 to 15 ingredients. By the time you've stepped out the door, your liver is already working through a sizeable chemical cocktail. And that's not counting anything you've eaten, drunk or taken in terms of medications, supplements or herbs.

HOW TO SUPPORT YOUR LIVER

- o Eat more fibre-rich vegetables, especially cruciferous ones like broccoli, cauliflower, kale, brussel-sprouts, bok choy, and watercress.
- o Have alcohol-free days.
- o Cut back on sugar, refined carbohydrates, high-fructose corn syrup, fruit juices, and fruit smoothies. These cause

sharp rises and falls in blood glucose and because the liver plays a central role in regulating blood sugar, repeated spikes and crashes can make it work much harder than it should.

o Swap unhealthy fats for healthy ones.

o Some medications, herbs, and supplements - like paracetamol, statins, iron, and vitamin A - can strain the liver if overused. Don't stop any prescribed medication but do speak with your doctor if you're unsure. It's always best to take only what you need and avoid self-prescribing.

If you're dealing with liver issues and constipation, make sure you're also supporting your large intestine and skin. They work closely alongside the liver.

YOUR LIVER AND ANGER

If many of your symptoms are pointing to your liver, take some time to look at how anger shows up in your life.

Do you often feel overwhelmed by anger or struggle with a short fuse? Are you easily irritated? Or do you avoid confrontation, stay silent when frustrated, or feel uncomfortable when others express anger? Maybe you rarely, if ever, get angry and pride yourself on keeping the peace.

However it shows up, it's worth getting curious about your relationship with this emotion.

Growing up, I never saw myself as an angry person. I didn't feel angry, and I certainly didn't have rage or temper issues. But I did have a liver disorder along with classic liver symptoms like fatigue, eye problems, and hormonal issues. I even had Hepatitis A as a teenager. Looking back, my body was trying to get my attention. The anger was there, just deeply buried.

Anger can be a difficult emotion to acknowledge but it's one that needs to be recognised and understood. None of our emotions are 'bad'. Love, joy, frustration, rage, jealousy, even hatred. These are all part of being human, and each one has something to teach us. Allow yourself to recognise, accept, and explore your anger. Let it help you learn about yourself.

Here are a few tips to help you release your anger a little.

Hit something

Years ago, a good friend of mine found out her husband was having an affair. She handled it with remarkable calm, asking him to leave and going through with a peaceful divorce for the sake of their young son. I admired her composure.

About a year later, she started experiencing chronic neck and shoulder pain and constipation. A massage therapist suggested she try releasing some of her tension - perhaps by hitting a pillow. She laughed while telling me this but then described what happened.

She went home, closed herself in her room, and gave her pillow a few awkward taps. She felt silly at first. Then she punched it a little harder. She still felt silly. Then a thought crossed her mind: "Imagine this is his face." Suddenly, something shifted. She hit the pillow harder. And harder. "And then," she said, "something took over and the next thing I knew, I'd completely shredded the pillow. Ripped it to bits. The stuffing was all over the room. I don't know what got into me."

I think it's more that her anger got out! And the interesting thing is that her health improved noticeably after that release.

Letting go of anger can be hard, especially in a world that praises self-control and sees big emotions as a sign of weakness. Feeling your anger can be especially difficult if you're the kind of person who tends to develop fatigue and are always trying to please others or keep the peace. Anger probably isn't an emotion you feel comfortable with.

But there are safe, healthy ways to feel and release anger without hurting anyone or causing a scene. Just like my friend did, punching a pillow can be a great start. Or try something more physical like boxing or kickboxing. One of my patients found kickboxing to be life changing. Not only did it help her release years of stored anger, it also gave her back a sense of strength she thought she'd lost.

What matters most is that you acknowledge the anger within you and take time to understand where it comes from. Acknowledge that it's a normal, healthy emotion and then allow yourself to feel and express it in a safe way.

If you don't give your anger space to be felt and released, it stays inside. It festers, twists, and eventually becomes destructive, either directed outward at others or inward toward your own body.

The angriest, most horrendous shingles eruption I've ever seen was in a well-presented, highly successful woman in her 40s. The rash was intense and centred around her anus. As we spoke, she revealed that she'd experienced sexual abuse in early childhood. She had kept this to herself for over 30 years and now it was coming out in her body.

The Two Chairs

When deep emotions have been held inside for years, especially when there was no safe space to express them, they start to show up in the body. Sometimes, just acknowledging what happened is healing in itself. Other times, we need a way to release what we couldn't say at the time.

The following exercise is one I sometimes share with patients to help them let go of anger or unspoken feelings, especially when it's not possible or safe to speak directly to the person who hurt them.

It can be helpful if you're carrying anger from childhood, grieving someone you never got to say goodbye to, or still holding pain from a parent who was absent, controlling, or emotionally closed off.

I'll walk you through the exercise now but please know you don't have to do it alone. A skilled counsellor or psychologist can sit alongside you and gently support you through the healing process.

Let's begin.

Step 1: Prepare Your Space

Set aside some quiet, unrushed time for this exercise. You'll need about an hour. When you're ready, go into a room where you feel safe, perhaps your bedroom or lounge. Close the door and place two chairs facing each other. Sit in one chair.

Step 2: Ground Yourself

Take a few moments to ground yourself and set your intention.

A simple way to do this is to sit quietly with your back straight and both feet flat on the floor. Close your eyes and begin by listening to the sounds outside - cars on the road, birds in the trees, maybe someone talking or watering their garden.

After a little while, bring your attention into the room. Notice any sounds - the ticking of a clock, your dog scratching, or perhaps just a lovely deep silence. Let yourself settle.

Then bring your attention to your body. Feel your feet on the ground. Feel how the chair supports you. Notice the air on your skin.

Turn your attention to your breath. Feel the air as it moves in and out of your nostrils. Can you sense the difference in temperature between the inhale and the exhale? Let your breath anchor you. Listen to it. Feel it moving through you.

Stay like this until you feel calm, supported, warm, and at peace.

Step 3: Set Your Intention

When you're ready, gently set your intention. Tell yourself why you're doing this exercise and what *you want to feel* at the end of it.

Hold onto that intention. It's the heart of the process.

Step 4: Invite Them In

The next steps might sound a bit strange at first but when you do them, you may be surprised by just how powerful and real they feel.

Sitting in your chair with your eyes closed, grounded and clear in your intention, begin to bring into your mind the person you want to speak to.

It might be someone who hurt or harmed you. It might be someone you hurt. It could be a loved one you never got to say goodbye to, or a parent you never truly knew.

Picture them sitting in the chair opposite you. Remember: you are safe, you are in control, and you are strong.

If you feel uneasy or alone, invite the image of someone who loves and supports you to stand behind you.

When I first did this exercise, I imagined both my brothers standing behind me. If you're spiritual or religious, you might picture your angels or guides with you. Let yourself feel held, supported, and protected.

Step 5: Start A Conversation

Now speak to the person in the other chair.

Say the words you never got to say. Let your heart speak freely. If you're angry, let them know. If you're hurt, let them know. If you're sorry, let them know.

Take as long as you need. Speak until you feel you've said enough.

When you're done, pause and take a few grounding breaths.

Step 6: Let Them Speak

Now gently stand up and move into the other chair. Sit in their chair and gently imagine being them, seeing you sitting opposite.

Speak as them. Say what they might have needed to say. Let them explain, or apologise, or simply express themselves.

Stay in this space for as long as you need. Let them speak fully.

Then give them a moment to breathe and be still.

Step 7: Let It Unfold

When they're finished, return to your original chair. If there's more to say, continue the conversation. Go back and forth as needed until everything feels complete.

Step 8: Come Back To Yourself

When the exchange feels finished, stay seated in your own chair. Be still.

Know that you are supported - by the chair, by your breath, by the love or presence you invited in.

Take some deep, steady breaths. Feel the breath moving through you. Let it settle you.

Slowly, bring your attention back to the room. Feel the chair beneath you. Feel your feet on the ground. Listen to the sounds around you, inside the room and beyond it.

When you're ready, open your eyes. Sit quietly. There's no rush.

To End: Acknowledge Your Courage

Before you get up, take a moment to acknowledge what you've been through. Wrap your arms around yourself and give yourself a hug. Not a quick one. A real, deep hug. Hold yourself.

This process takes courage. It's not easy to sit with pain, to speak what's been unsaid, or to feel what you've been carrying. But you did it. You showed up for yourself in a brave and honest way.

Say to yourself: *Well done. I'm proud of you.* Acknowledge your courage. Let this hug be a way of saying: *I'm here. I've got you. You're not alone.*

In The Days Ahead

Over the next few days, a lot of emotions will start to bubble up. This is okay. Let them come.

This is a really good time to journal, go for long walks in nature, have a deeply cleansing swim, take long relaxing baths and rest.

Let life unravel. Let what will be, be. You don't have to control everything, and you don't have to change anything. You've done enough.

B, YOUR KIDNEYS

Buried in fat and no bigger than a bar of soap, your kidneys quietly filter and clean your blood, and balance its volume, composition, pH, and pressure. Unfortunately, these hard-working organs are delicate and easily affected by chronic conditions and naturally decline with age. That's why it's important to care for them.

HOW TO SUPPORT YOUR KIDNEYS

High blood pressure, diabetes, stress, excess sugar, smoking, and overusing painkillers (like NSAIDs) can all harm your kidneys over time. If you're noticing kidney-related symptoms, it doesn't necessarily mean you have kidney disease but it may mean your kidneys are under pressure and could use some support.

A simple way to care for them is to focus on three things: easing stress, steadying blood sugars, and using medicines and supplements only as prescribed.

Stress often drives high blood pressure, which strains the kidneys. Get curious about your stress and practise small, regular resets; you'll find plenty of ideas throughout this book. Diabetes mellitus often develops after long-term blood-sugar imbalance; for practical steps to stabilise your sugars, revisit Chapter 3. And stay aware of potential side-effects or interactions from any medications, herbs or supplements you take. Chat to your prescribing doctor if you're at all concerned.

YOUR KIDNEYS AND FEAR

If you're experiencing symptoms related to your kidneys, take a moment to reflect on how the emotion of fear might be showing up in your life.

Do you often feel unsafe or on edge? Did you grow up afraid of someone or something? Or do you lean the other way - bold, seemingly fearless, even a bit of a daredevil?

Anger can also be a clue. Often there's fear sitting quietly beneath it, with anger stepping in to protect you from what feels unsafe. If anger is familiar, you might gently ask whether a softer fear is hiding underneath.

Emotions such as fear and anger are here to protect us. Try to get to know them. Explore them through speed-writing, journalling, or even by taking a long walk and allowing your mind to wander. Think back to when these emotions first began. What situation were you in? Who was around you, where were you living, and what was happening in your life at the time? You'll likely begin to see that these emotions once played an important role in helping you cope and stay safe.

Now, ask yourself if you still need them? Consider where you are right now in your life. Today. Do you still need to be afraid, hyperalert, on edge all the time? Do you still need to be defensive, angry, judgemental, critical? Are fear and anger still serving you?

If not, then thank them for all the help and support they've given you in your journey and let them go.

If you feel you still need them, if you don't yet feel safe or secure, then that's okay. Allow those emotions to stay with you and protect you but do start recognising them when they surface. Say hello them!

Interestingly, we often don't realise how deeply we were caught up in an emotion until we've stepped out of it. My husband and I had our children in South Africa, where high-security measures were just part of life - barbed wire, security beams, floodlights, metal gates, panic buttons, and armed response. It felt normal at the time.

When we moved to Australia, we moved into a house with no fence, no security doors, not even burglar guards on the windows. We felt so insecure in our new house we could hardly sleep! Looking back, I can see just how deeply fear and insecurity had shaped our lives in South Africa. No wonder we were so exhausted.

If you've been through trauma, I encourage you to work with a counsellor or therapist to support your healing. It can be a slow and sometimes difficult process but releasing emotional pain and past trauma will bring a profound shift in your health and energy. A handful of supplements or green juices won't get you there. You really do need to go deeper.

C, YOUR LUNGS

Your lungs have a surface area the size of a tennis court, and every single cell in your body depends on them. Without oxygen, there's no energy. Without breath, there's no life.

You're probably familiar with the usual respiratory symptoms - coughs, colds, blocked noses, sinusitis, and postnasal drip. We all go through them from time to time, and that's completely normal. But if these symptoms linger, keep returning, or don't respond to treatment, it might be time to look a little deeper.

How to support your Lungs

Please always work with a medical professional if you have breathing difficulties or any kind of lung infection. The suggestions below are not intended to treat medical conditions. They're offered for general support only.

Breathe deeply

Most of us breathe shallowly without even realising it, especially when we're stressed or caught in fight-or-flight mode. We tend to rely on our upper chest and shoulder muscles rather than fully engaging our diaphragms and this not only keeps our bodies on high alert but also adds to neck and shoulder tension. Over time, shallow breathing limits lung expansion and reduces the efficiency of oxygen exchange.

By slowing down and practising deep breathing, you can gently guide your body back into a more relaxed state while also supporting your lungs and overall respiratory health. Deep, steady breaths allow your lungs to expand more fully, strengthen the breathing muscles, and improve oxygen delivery throughout your body. To try this, imagine a soft balloon in your belly. As you breathe in through your nose, let your belly rise as though the balloon is filling with air. Then exhale slowly, allowing the belly to soften back in. Repeat a few times, either lying on your back or sitting upright, whichever feels most comfortable to you.

Spending just a few minutes each day focusing on slow, deep breathing can make a real difference. Practices like yoga, Tai Chi, and structured breathwork can also help retrain old patterns and restore healthier, more natural breathing rhythms. And if you live with a chronic lung condition such as COPD, you may find the Buteyko Technique especially valuable. In the Bibliography, I've recommended an excellent book by Patrick McKeown.

Reduce mucous-forming foods

If you often struggle with respiratory conditions coupled with a blocked nose or postnasal drip, it may help to reduce foods that are known to thicken mucous. For example, dairy and fried foods. There's an old saying that "milk makes mucous" and while dairy doesn't necessarily increase how much mucous your body produces, it can make it thicker and harder to clear, leaving you more prone to congestion and infection.

If giving up dairy feels difficult, there are simple ways to make it easier on your system. Warming milk and adding a small pinch of black pepper - an approach rooted in Ayurveda - can help reduce its mucous-thickening effects and make it more tolerable.

Support your large intestine

In Traditional Chinese Medicine (TCM), the lungs and large intestine are considered closely linked, and when one is out of balance, the other is often affected. For example, weak lung energy is thought to contribute to constipation, and sluggish digestion can, in turn, weaken the lungs.

Interestingly, this also makes sense physiologically. The diaphragm - the main muscle of breathing - sits between the lungs and the large intestine, and it plays a central role in both respiration and peristalsis, the wave-like movement that carries food through the colon. When we don't breathe deeply, constipation can become more likely; and when we're constipated, it can be harder to take full, deep breaths.

So if you are struggling with a respiratory condition, remember to also support your large intestine (I'll explore this in more detail in the coming pages).

YOUR LUNGS AND SADNESS

Both the lungs and the large intestine are associated with grief and the inability to let go. In particular, the lungs are linked with sadness and unexpressed sorrow. You may have heard the sayings, "mucous is the tears we haven't cried," or "post-nasal drip is the sadness we keep swallowing." When grief is unspoken, it doesn't disappear. Instead it finds other ways to make itself known in the body.

I've seen this pattern often in my work. For years, my practice focused on cancer care, and time after time, I noticed a pattern: women with breast cancer had often experienced deep emotional loss - whether from the death of a loved one, the end of a marriage, or the upheaval of immigration.

Just last week, I saw an elderly client with silicosis. He'd worked as a tiler, so the physical cause was clear. But I found myself wondering: why him, and not his colleagues? When I gently mentioned that our lungs can hold onto grief, he opened up about how lonely he felt, and how much it hurt that his children never visited.

Many of us struggle to talk about loss. We keep busy, swallow our sadness, and push through. But grief doesn't vanish when ignored. It settles in our lungs, our hearts, and our chests.

If you've lost someone or something you love, give yourself the space to feel that loss. Grieving is not something to rush or push aside - healing begins by allowing yourself to fully acknowledge what you feel. Letting go starts with letting yourself grieve.

If you feel ready, a simple ritual can help you mark the moment of letting go. It doesn't have to be elaborate - small, intentional acts can hold deep healing power. What matters most is the meaning they carry for you personally.

Here are some gentle rituals that may support you through the process. Choose what resonates with you and let it be symbolic of releasing your sadness in a way that feels safe and meaningful.

Say Goodbye

Choose something that represents the person, event, or experience you're holding onto. Place it in nature, bury it, or release it into water. As you do, allow yourself to say "thank you" and "goodbye."

When I was in the depths of my fatigue, I lost five loved ones in just three months. It was overwhelming. One day, I took five of my favourite shells down to the beach and, one by one, threw them into the ocean. It was painful, but it was also something I deeply needed to do.

Write and Release

Writing can be a powerful way to give voice to what cannot be spoken. Write a letter to the person, situation, or part of your life you are ready to let go of. Say everything you need to say. Then let it go symbolically. Burn it, bury it, or tear it up and throw it away. Whichever you choose, let it symbolize you're letting go.

Honour Their Presence

If you've lost someone dear and are struggling to cope with the idea that they're no longer here, find something beautiful to represent them and place it somewhere in your home where you'll see it often.

I have a small crystal in my lounge that represents my dad. Every time I see it, I'm reminded that his energy is still with me. I don't have to focus on the fact that he's not here in person. I can hold on to his presence, not his absence.

D, YOUR SKIN

Your skin is the largest organ in your body and acts as the interface between you and your world. It's a fascinating organ. While it can be as thin as 0.5mm, the average adult's skin weighs nearly 5kg!

Your skin also serves as a kind of barometer for your wellbeing. It often reflects what's going on inside and shows whether you're eating poorly, are dehydrated, not sleeping well, or under stress.

Ohashi writes:

"Many of us regard sensitive skin as a curse, but in fact it is a blessing. Sensitive skin can be very beautiful, but only if you live in harmony with the external environment. You must eat the foods that suit your health and the health of your skin. If you do not, your appearance will be affected. In this way, the universe uses our vanity to guide us toward good health...I consider that those who can eat all sorts of unhealthful foods and still look good are the ones that are in trouble, because their barometer cannot be used to guide them towards better health."

Take a moment to look at your own skin. What is it trying to tell you?

If you've got acne or frequent breakouts, your body may be signalling that it's time to cut back on sugar, deep-fried foods, and processed junk. It's also worth supporting your liver and large intestine, as they play a key role in detoxification. If your skin is reactive and hypersensitive, think eczema or hives, it's another sign to support your liver and gut.

It may also be time to ask yourself: who or what is irritating me? Where might I need clearer personal boundaries? Your skin is not just a physical barrier - it's the actual interface between you and the rest of the world. It's both a boundary and a communication point. When it's flaring up, it's worth reflecting on whether you're saying "yes" in areas of your life where you'd rather say "no."

I find it so interesting how when parents bring in their little baby with eczema, it often points me towards boundary struggles in the parents' own lives. The baby's skin can sometimes be a gentle signal for me to check in with the parents and explore what's happening for them - whether that's stress in their relationship, challenges with grandparents, or pressures at work.

The colour of your skin also reflects your health. If you're unusually pale then you need to look at how well oxygenated your tissues are – are you perhaps anaemic or do you have a respiratory disorder? If your skin is yellowish you may be jaundiced which can suggest you need to look more deeply at the health of your liver. These are issues you will need to see your doctor for.

One last thing: as you move forward on your healing journey and begin releasing old imbalances, toxins, or emotions, it's quite normal to experience a few skin eruptions. Everything buried within you is now surfacing. Pimples, rashes, or flare-ups can be part of the clearing process. If they last just a few days, try not to suppress them. Let everything come out. However, if you're at all worried please do see a healthcare practitioner.

E, YOUR LARGE INTESTINE

I've left the large intestine till last because it's all about 'letting go'.

If you're struggling with fatigue and symptoms related to your liver, lungs or skin, then there's a good chance you're holding on to emotions and not letting go of old stuff that no longer serves you.

Beliefs, thought patterns, fear, anger, grief - all that stuff that may have helped you once but that's now just keeping you down. Stuff you're carrying around. Heavy stuff. Stuff that's eating up your energy and making you tired.

Think about it - constipation is your body's inability to let go of its waste. What waste are you hanging on to? What don't you need anymore?

HOW TO SUPPORT YOUR LARGE INTESTINE

Alongside paying attention to what you eat, try starting your day with a 'mini-cleanse'. Begin each morning with a mug of hot water on an empty stomach and wait 20–30 minutes before eating or drinking anything else. If you like, add a thin slice of lemon.

Also be aware that gentle movement can make a real difference to digestive health. A walk in the sunshine, paired with slow, steady breathing, helps stimulate healthy bowel function. Restorative or yin yoga can also be very supportive, especially if you ask your teacher to guide you through poses that aid digestion. Abdominal massage, when done by a trained therapist, is another powerful tool. And deep belly breathing supports the natural movement of food through your intestines and helps your body to eliminate waste.

Your Large Intestine and Holding On

How do you let go of emotions you've carried for years? How do you release thoughts or beliefs that once helped you survive but now weigh you down?

The suggestions below have been helpful for many, but I want to gently remind you - healing takes time. Be patient and kind with yourself. The answers don't always come quickly, and each step may take days, weeks, or even months. Just know this: if you're willing to move forward, and willing to let go, you will.

Practice Stillness

I say "practice" because stillness doesn't come from flipping a switch. It takes time, and it needs to be nurtured daily.

Revisit Chapter 13 and start letting go of the things that no longer serve you. That includes all the tasks on your to-do list you don't really want to do. By doing less, you create space for what truly matters.

Clear your environment too. Let go of objects, clothes, and clutter you no longer love or need. You'll find that releasing physical things can make it easier to release emotional ones too.

168

And then, begin setting aside just a few minutes each day to be still. Five to ten minutes is enough. What matters is that you do it regularly.

Sit quietly on a bench and listen to the busy world around you. Snuggle up in the corner of your couch and watch the steam coming off your coffee. Go for a walk in the park without your earphones in. No music, no podcasts, no audiobooks. Simply you.

Build Awareness

It's important to become aware of what you're holding onto and to gently explore why.

I've found that journaling, asking myself honest questions, and taking long walks in nature help me uncover what I'm carrying and why it's still there.

Be patient with yourself. The answers don't always arrive quickly, but they will come at the right time. Your job is simply to keep building awareness, to keep gently digging inward. As Peter Drucker said, "The important and difficult job is never to find the right answers. It is to find the right question."

Start with questions: What am I holding onto? Is it helping me or holding me back? If it's no longer serving me, am I ready to let it go?

Create a Ritual

Conditions of the large intestine often mirror the things we struggle to release - grief, resentment, or old stories we keep carrying. A simple ritual can help you acknowledge these feelings and gently signal to your body and mind that it's safe to let go. It doesn't need to be elaborate; what matters most is the meaning it holds for you. Even the smallest, intentional gesture done with awareness can become a way of releasing what no longer serves you. If you'd like inspiration, turn back to the lung section, where I shared two gentle rituals: "*Say Goodbye*" and "*Write and Release*".

169

Ho'oponopono: A Practice of Making It Right

Ho'oponopono is without a doubt one of the hardest, most deeply moving exercises I have ever done.

Based on the Hawaiian tradition of making it right, it encourages you to forgive and let go and reminds us that sometimes the person we most need to forgive is ourselves.

Start with a short speed writing exercise. Set your timer for 60 seconds. Grab a pen and paper and quickly write down:

- o   Names of anyone who has hurt you - people, events, or situations that left you feeling betrayed, humiliated, or deeply upset.
- o   Names of anyone you feel you may have hurt or let down.
- o   Don't overthink it. Aim for at least ten names.

Then choose one name from your list. Start with someone or something that feels easiest to forgive or let go of.

- o   Close your eyes and visualise the person. When you see them clearly in your mind, say their name and then repeat the following phrases (either aloud or silently):
- o   I love you
- o   I thank you
- o   I forgive you / Please forgive me
- o   I'm sorry.

Keep repeating these phrases until you feel you're saying them with depth and honesty. Work through each person on your list one at a time. As you say each phrase, try to give a reason for your words. For example, when you say "I love you," add why. When you say "I thank you," explain what for. Once you've worked through the easier ones, you'll likely feel more energy to face the harder ones.

This might sound simple, but it can be incredibly difficult, especially if someone has hurt you deeply. How do you say "I love you" or "I thank you" to someone who makes your blood run cold? And why should you say "I'm sorry" to them?

I can't answer that for you but I believe you already hold the answers within. Whatever pain was caused, ask yourself: did anything good come from it? Did I grow? Did I learn something new about myself? Look deeper. Then deeper still.

There may be someone you're not ready, or able, to forgive. That's okay. You can adapt the exercise. Instead of saying "I forgive you," "I thank you," or "I love you," try saying, "I want to be able to forgive you" or "I want to be able to thank you."

Remember, this exercise is for you. It's part of your healing journey and your process of letting go. It's not really about the other person. It's about releasing what you no longer want to carry.

This can be a very painful exercise, but it's also deeply transformational. If you want to create more energy in your life, you need to let go of what weighs you down. As Katrina Mayer beautifully puts it, "Get rid of clutter and you may just find it was blocking the door you've been looking for".

GENERAL HEALTHY HABITS

Getting to know and release your emotions really is a journey. And truthfully, I don't have all the answers. I'm still on that path myself. What I've found is that just when you think you've dealt with something, another layer tends to surface.

It reminds me of a story in Ryan Holiday's *Ego is the Enemy*. He writes about a martial artist who said training is like sweeping a floor: you can't do it once and expect it to stay clean. The dust always comes back. So you sweep again. And again.

I've come to see that life isn't about having a spotless room, but about what you learn and gain each time you sweep. And when the work of letting go emotionally feels too heavy or exhausting, step back and anchor in something physical. Remember, your body is constantly working quietly in the background, clearing away what it no longer needs so you can move through life with more ease. Supporting your organs of elimination is one of the simplest, most practical ways to help this process along.

The small, everyday habits below may seem ordinary, but they create a steady foundation for energy and balance. Think of them as simple practices that help your body release what it doesn't need and make space for what it does need. In the end, letting go - whether physically or emotionally - is what keeps things moving forward.

- o **Eat plenty of vegetables** – they're rich in fibre to keep things moving and packed with antioxidants that protect your cells.
- o **Move your body every day** – even a gentle walk makes a difference.
- o **Sweat often** – sweating through exercise or sauna helps your skin release waste, improves circulation, and eases the load on your kidneys. If you have heart concerns, check with your doctor first, and if you're fatigued, start slowly.
- o **Drink clean, filtered water** – it's one of the simplest ways to support your system.
- o **Keep your blood sugars steady** – avoid big spikes and crashes by balancing meals with protein, healthy fats, and fibre.
- o **Practise deep breathing** – it not only calms your nervous system but also helps your body clear waste more efficiently.
- o **Try dry body brushing** – gently brush your dry skin with a natural bristle brush before showering, moving in long strokes from your hands and feet towards your heart. This supports circulation and stimulates lymphatic flow, helping your body clear waste and strengthen immunity.

o **Eat antioxidant-rich foods** – nuts, berries, plums, and citrus fruits all bring colour and protective compounds to your diet.

o **Minimise plastic contact with food and drinks** – store leftovers in glass containers and avoid heating food in plastic.

Also, be aware of the many ways environmental toxins can creep into daily life and burden your organs of elimination. They may be present in the food you eat, the water you drink, the products you use on your skin, or even the air inside your home. While it's impossible to avoid every source, becoming more conscious of them allows you to make small, practical choices that reduce your exposure. Over time, these small shifts can ease the burden and support your body's natural ability to stay balanced.

Be mindful of what's in your:

o **Household cleaners** – many everyday sprays and detergents are full of strong chemicals that add to the load your body has to deal with. Choosing simpler or natural options can make a real difference over time.

o **Fish and seafood** – larger fish such as shark, swordfish and some types of tuna can contain higher levels of mercury, while smaller fish like sardines, anchovies, and mackerel are usually much lower. You don't need to cut fish out altogether, but it's wise to choose the smaller, lower-mercury varieties more often. When you can, opt for wild-caught fish, as they generally carry fewer contaminants than farmed ones.

o **Air quality** – the air inside your home can sometimes be more polluted than the air outside. Check your air conditioner is clean, you're letting fresh air in by opening windows, and also think about what kinds of products you're using indoors.

o **Garden products** – pesticides, herbicides, and fungicides are common, but they can affect both your health and the environment. Look for gentler alternatives where you can.

o **Skincare and cosmetics** – the products you put on your skin every day can carry hidden chemicals. Shampoos, deodorants, soaps, toothpastes, hair dyes, and nail polish often contain additives like parabens, phthalates, SLS, or even traces of heavy metals. Reading labels and choosing cleaner alternatives where you can helps ease the load on your system. Remember, your skin absorbs much of what you put on it, which is why I like the saying: *"only put on your skin what you would eat."*

o **Workplace chemicals** – if your job involves handling solvents, paints, or other industrial chemicals, it's worth making sure you have proper protective equipment.

o **Living spaces** – mould in the home is easy to overlook but can have a big impact on your health. It's worth checking regularly, especially in damp areas.

SLOWLY, GENTLY, FORWARD

I don't really know how to end this book, except by saying that if you've made it to here – well done! And I hope that, if you've taken anything from it, it's the quiet knowing that, as Christopher Robin once said: "You are braver than you believe, stronger than you seem, and smarter than you think."

You may not feel "healed." You may still feel tired. That's okay. This isn't the end - it's a new kind of beginning.

You now carry insight you didn't have before. You've met parts of yourself you'd forgotten. You've opened up space.

The energy will come. Slowly and gently.

Just keep moving forward.

TOOLS & RESOURCES

I've gone back and forth about whether to include the following in this book. Part of me hesitated, because I don't want you to turn only to herbs or homoeopathic remedies for your fatigue without also tending to the deeper work of letting go of old emotions, nourishing yourself, and gently shifting the habits that keep you stuck.

In the end, I've chosen to include it because I know how valuable a little extra support can be when you're running on empty. Please just remember: these remedies are not a replacement for true healing. They are simply here to offer support while you do the deeper work.

I'm sharing only a small selection of herbs and remedies that are safe to use at home. There is so much more that herbalism and homoeopathy can offer, and I encourage you to seek out a qualified practitioner who can walk alongside you on your journey.

Homoeopathic Support For Fatigue

I only came to study homoeopathy in my thirties. After nearly ten years of struggling with fatigue - and trying every diet, supplement, and health protocol I could find - it was homoeopathy that finally turned my health around on a deep and lasting level. That's why I fell so completely in love with it.

Homoeopathy has many healing pathways: nosodes to help you recover from infections, miasmatic remedies to shift long-held patterns, and constitutional remedies to nurture and rebuild your energy. What I'm offering here is just a taste of a few easily available remedies. They won't work as deeply as a constitutional or miasmatic remedy, but they do offer gentle support for specific symptoms. My hope is that it inspires you to explore further and seek out a homoeopath to support you in your healing journey.

A Few Important Notes Before You Start

If you're new to homoeopathy, it may seem strange at first because it works quite differently to Western medicine. While Western medicine often focuses on removing, replacing, or killing what's "wrong," homoeopathy works on a more subtle level, supporting the body's energy so it can restore its own balance.

Instead of forcing change, we use tiny doses of a remedy to gently nudge the body's energy back into harmony. That's why you only need a small dose and not too often. Your body does the healing once it's pointed in the right direction.

The remedies below can help with fatigue. Choose just one remedy at a time, and give it space to work before trying another and take a dose only when needed – sometimes once or twice is enough. If symptoms return, repeat as necessary, but always pause and observe. With homoeopathy, less is more.

HOMOEOPATHY FOR GRIEF & LOSS

Grief and loss often sit quietly beneath deep fatigue. And it's not always the obvious losses - sometimes it's the loss of a loved one or a relationship, but it can also be the loss of a job, a dream, your sense of identity, the heartbreak of losing a baby during pregnancy, or the deep ache of homesickness after immigration.

The remedies below may offer gentle support. Try a 30CH once daily for 3–5 days. If your grief feels complex or long-held, I encourage you to reach out to a qualified homoeopath or counsellor for deeper support.

- o **Ignatia amara** – A beautiful remedy for recent, sudden grief, especially when emotions are unpredictable. You might be tearful one moment, numb the next, sighing often, or trying hard to hold everything in. Ignatia can help soften that raw, aching place.
- o **Natrum muriaticum** – This remedy often helps when grief has been carried quietly for a long time. If you tend to keep your feelings to yourself, don't like to cry in front of others, and have a history of heartbreak or loss, Nat Mur can gently unlock what's been held inside. If tears come, let them. You'll feel lighter for it.
- o **Phosphoric acid** – When grief becomes layered by one loss after another and you feel completely drained, Phos Ac may help. It's for that state where you feel flat, disconnected, and too tired to cry.

HOMOEOPATHY FOR INSOMNIA

In my experience, a well-matched constitutional remedy prescribed by a qualified homoeopath is the most effective solution to insomnia. But to get started, you could try one of these remedies:

- Arsenicum album – If you wake shortly after midnight and lie there restless and anxious, unable to switch off, this may help. You might also feel chilly, exhausted from even small tasks, and find your thoughts racing with worry. Or your dreams may be full of cares and worries.
- Bellis perennis – This remedy can be helpful when you're feeling overworked, worn out or struggling with post-exertional malaise. It's especially useful if you wake early each morning and can't fall back asleep. It can also help with that bruised, sore feeling you may get from overdoing things.
- Coffea cruda – If your mind feels like it's had too much coffee - wide awake, overstimulated, and buzzing with thoughts when you're meant to be sleeping - try Coffea 30CH before bed for a few nights. I sometimes pop a pilule into a glass of water and keep it by my bedside, so if I wake in the night and can't get back to sleep, I can just take a sip.

HOMOEOPATHY FOR ACHES & PAINS

Fibromyalgia, muscle stiffness, and joint pain are common with fatigue. Here are a few remedies that may offer some relief:

- Arnica montana – If you find that every time you exercise you feel bruised, sore, and unable to sleep afterwards, try a dose of Arnica 30CH after activity. It can also help after long flights or car trips when your body feels sore and bruised.
- Bryonia alba – If your joint pain feels sharp, tearing, or stitching and gets worse with any movement, Bryonia may be the remedy for you.
- Kalium carbonicum – This remedy is especially helpful for tired people with back pain and a deep sense of

weakness. The pain tends to feel sharp or cutting, improves with movement, and worsens with rest. You may also notice increased perspiration.

- o **Rhus toxicodendron** – If you feel stiff, sore, and achy first thing in the morning or after a rest, but loosen up and improve once you start moving, then try some Rhus tox. You may also feel worse when cold and much better after a warm bath or shower.

Herbal Support For Fatigue

When it comes to fatigue, I'm not a fan of supplements so haven't recommended any in this book. They might give you a little boost, but unless you're also changing your diet and lifestyle, that energy won't last. I know this from experience. When I was deeply fatigued, I used to give myself weekly vitamin B injections just to get through the week. It helped for a while and then I'd crash. It was like a sugar hit or strong coffee and long-term it made me worse, not better, because it gave me energy to keep running around doing things when I really should have been resting.

However, I do love herbs. They're nutrient-rich, gentle, and the body knows what to do with them. Below you'll find a list of the herbs that I most often use with patients struggling with fatigue. They are gentle, slow-acting herbs so you won't notice a big difference at first but know that they will be working in the background to feed, nourish and support your energy.

A Few Important Notes Before You Start

I highly recommend working with a qualified herbalist. The herbs I've listed here are generally safe if you're not taking any other medications, but if you are, it's important to check for potential interactions. A qualified herbalist can guide you, recommend a safe blend tailored to your needs, and adjust it as your body responds.

If you're taking medication and choose to use these herbs without the guidance of a herbalist, it's important to have your medication monitored by your doctor as some herbs can change the way your body processes medication.

It's also essential to use high-quality herbs - another good reason to visit a herbalist. Always choose organic herbs and avoid cheap options online as you can't be sure of their quality. Some of the herbs mentioned below can be grown in a pot on your kitchen windowsill or in your garden.

The easiest way to use most herbs is as a tea or a tincture. Avoid capsules or pills, as they often contain unnecessary fillers which can aggravate your gut.

Don't try everything listed below. Choose just one or two herbs at a time, use them for a few weeks and then move onto a different one if you need.

And finally, a word on dosage:

This may sound counterintuitive, but if you're feeling very tired, it's best to avoid large amounts of herbs. Instead, use small "drop doses." For example, if you're taking a tincture, try 3 drops in water, 3 times a day rather than the full recommended dose. The same goes for herbal teas: 1–2 cups per day is better than the usual 3–5. When your body is exhausted, it needs gentle, nourishing support, not stimulation or 'false energy.' I hope that makes sense.

Also, most of the herbs below are best used short term. Try one for 10-14 days then reassess. Your body should have shifted during that time.

MEET THE HERBS

ALFALFA (MEDICAGO SATIVA)

Rich in vitamins, minerals, and chlorophyll, Alfalfa is a gentle, nourishing tonic for the whole body. It's especially helpful when fatigue is linked to poor nutrition, anaemia, or slow recovery from illness. As a mild phytoestrogen, it can also support women during menopause. Avoid if you're on blood-thinning medication or immunosuppressants. Take 3-5 drops in a little water, 2-3 times daily, away from food. Combines well with Nettles, Milky Oats and Withania.

DANDELION LEAF AND ROOT (TARAXACUM OFFICINALE)

My favourite herbalist, Margaret Roberts, recommends eating three fresh dandelion leaves a day - I try to! These little weeds, so often pulled out of gardens, are among the most nourishing, detoxifying, and strengthening herbs you'll find. The leaves are rich in easily absorbable vitamins and minerals (especially calcium), while the roots support liver detoxification and stimulate digestion. It also supports the liver in processing hormones, making it particularly helpful if your fatigue is linked to PMS, period problems, or perimenopause - or if you tend to feel more tired around ovulation. If you're eating the leaves fresh, chop them finely and add a little salt to reduce their bitterness then toss into salads or stir-fries. Dandelion root 'coffee' is available in most health shops, or you can use the tincture: 3–5 drops in a little water, 2–3 times daily. Dandelion pairs beautifully with Nettles for a nutrient boost.

LEMON BALM (MELISSA OFFICINALIS)

Such a beautiful, gentle herb for anxiety, low mood, and trouble sleeping. It also soothes digestive issues, especially when they're linked to stress or worry. Lemon Balm is best used fresh, so try growing some in your garden (the bees will thank you!). To make a tea, use ¼ cup of fresh sprigs with 1 cup of boiling water. Let it stand for 5 minutes before drinking. If you don't like herbal teas, cool it and use as a base for juice.

LIQUORICE ROOT (GLYCYRRHIZA GLABRA)

One of my favourite herbs for people recovering from long-term stress or adrenal burnout. Liquorice gently supports adrenal and thyroid function, helps raise low blood pressure, and soothes the digestive tract. It's also anti-inflammatory and nourishing, helping the body cope with stress while calming inflammation and supporting immunity. It works best when combined with other herbs, helping to balance and enhance formulas. Avoid if you have high blood pressure or are on medication for hypertension.

MILKY OATS (AVENA SATIVA)

Rich in B-vitamins as well as minerals, oats are deeply nourishing, especially if you're struggling with long-term stress, anxiety or grief. They slowly, gently help calm and restore your nervous system. They also support the thyroid gland and are particularly helpful if you're going through menopause. Best taken as a fresh tincture, 3–5 drops in a little warm water, 2–3 times a day. Combines beautifully with Withania or Lemon Balm.

NETTLES (URTICA DIOICA)

Another garden weed you should be eating, not pulling out! Nettles are a wonderful all-round tonic - cleansing and detoxifying the whole body, soothing allergies, building strength, and boosting iron levels. Add the fresh leaves to soups and stews or enjoy as a tea every second day (avoid daily use long-term). To make a tea, steep ¼ cup of fresh sprigs in 1 cup of hot water for 5 minutes.

PASSIONFLOWER (PASSIFLORA INCARNATA)

Herbalist Phyllis Light calls Passionflower her number one herb for post-traumatic stress, and I've found it to be a gentle, calming support for deep fatigue and trauma-related insomnia. Look for a tincture made from the fresh plant and take 3–5 drops in a little water, 2–3 times a day, or just before bed. It helps quiet a racing mind and combines beautifully with Lemon Balm for anxiety, Milky Oats for nervous exhaustion, and Withania for long-term stress.

ROSEMARY (ROSMARINUS OFFICINALIS)

Known as the 'herb of remembrance', Rosemary is my go-to when I'm feeling flat and foggy-brained. It gives a gentle mental boost, helps bring clarity, is energising and also eases tension headaches, soothes joint pain, and supports recovery from long-term stress. Enjoy it as a tea every second day, add fresh sprigs to your cooking, or take 3 drops of tincture in a little water when needed. Combines well with Dandelion Root to help detoxify and restore energy. Avoid if you have high blood pressure and do not use long term.

WITHANIA (ASHWAGANDHA – WITHANIA SOMNIFERA)

This is probably the herb I reach for most often when it comes to fatigue. It's especially helpful when you feel 'wired but tired' or just too exhausted to sleep. You know that feeling! Withania gently supports both the thyroid and adrenal glands. It's an adaptogen, which means it can calm you when you're feeling anxious and lift you when you're feeling low. It also helps relax tight, tense muscles and rebuild strength when you're feeling depleted. Withania is one of the few herbs that can be taken long-term (up to 3 months), but it may interact with some medications. So it's best to keep the dose low - just 3 drops, 2–3 times a day - and have your medications monitored by your doctor.

HERBS FOR ANAEMIA OR LOW IRON

- Alfalfa
- Nettles
- Herbs For Low Blood Pressure
- Liquorice root
- Rosemary
- Withania

HERBS FOR THYROID & ADRENAL SUPPORT

Please see your doctor, herbalist, or homoeopath to have your thyroid properly assessed and managed. These herbs are here to gently support, not replace, any prescribed treatment.

- Liquorice root
- Withania

HERBS FOR BRAIN FOG, MEMORY PROBLEMS & BURNOUT

- Milky oats
- Rosemary
- Withania

HERBS FOR ANXIETY, STRESS & INSOMNIA

- Alfalfa
- Lemon balm
- Milky oats
- Passionflower
- Withania

HERBS FOR DIGESTION & LIVER

- o Dandelion root
- o Dandelion leaf
- o Lemon balm
- o Liquorice root
- o Nettles
- o Rosemary

HERBS TO NOURISH & REBUILD YOU

- o Alfalfa
- o Dandelion leaf
- o Milky oats
- o Nettles
- o Withania

A Simple Food Guide

I think this is a good place to pause and take a breath. We've covered a lot in the last few chapters, so here's a simple recap, along with a few extra suggestions, to help you put everything into practice. These food guidelines are designed to support blood sugar balance, calm inflammation, nourish your microbiome, and gently begin rebuilding your energy.

Eat at Least Two Cups Of Vegetables With Every Meal

Vegetables are packed with vitamins, minerals, and antioxidants essential for health. They help balance blood sugar, keep your digestive system moving with fibre, and feed your microbiome.

Aim to eat at least two cups, or half a plateful, of vegetables with every meal. Mix it up and buy different vegetables each time you shop to help you get variety in your diet.

Be Careful With Fruit

Fruit is rich in fibre, vitamins, minerals, and antioxidants but it quickly increases your blood sugars. Don't eat fruit alone otherwise you'll be back on the blood sugar roller-coaster. Always eat fruit together with a protein or fat and avoid fruit juices and fruit smoothies – rather go for vegetable ones.

INCLUDE A HEALTHY FAT WITH EVERY MEAL

Good fats help balance your blood sugars, calm inflammation and nourish your brain. They're also the building blocks of many hormones, support the absorption of vitamins A, D, E, and K, and form an essential part of every cell in your body. Try to eat more:

- **Extra Virgin Olive Oil**
  Rich in monounsaturated fats and powerful antioxidants, olive oil helps reduce inflammation throughout the body. Use it cold in salads or in gentle low-heat cooking.

- **Oily Fish (e.g. salmon, sardines, mackerel, anchovies)**
  Packed with omega-3 fatty acids (EPA and DHA), oily fish reduce the production of inflammatory compounds. Omega-3s are also crucial for brain function.

- **Nuts (e.g. walnuts, almonds, macadamias)**
  Nuts contain healthy fats, vitamin E, and other antioxidants that help lower inflammation. Walnuts are especially high in omega-3s.

- **Seeds (e.g. flaxseeds, chia seeds, hemp seeds)**
  These little powerhouses are rich in alpha-linolenic acid (ALA), a plant-based omega-3 that helps calm inflammation. Ground flaxseed or chia in smoothies is a great option. And if you're menopausal, flaxseeds can help calm your hot flushes!

- **Avocados**
  Full of monounsaturated fats, fibre, and anti-inflammatory compounds, avocados support both heart and brain health.

- **Ghee or Grass-Fed Butter (in moderation)**
  Though technically saturated fats, these contain anti-inflammatory compounds and can be used for cooking at high temperatures due to their heat stability.

EAT PROTEIN WITH EVERY MEAL

Protein is critical to good health. It's needed to build and repair tissues, produce enzymes and hormones essential to both physical and mental health, and it plays a vital role in the immune system. Eating protein with every meal also helps balance your blood sugars and fermented proteins such as tempeh or yoghurt feed your microbiome.

Animal Sources

- Meat (beef, lamb, pork, game)
- Poultry (chicken, turkey)
- Fish & seafood (salmon, sardines, mackerel, tuna, prawns, mussels, oysters)
- Eggs
- Dairy (milk, yoghurt, cheese)

Plant Sources

- Soy-based products (tofu, tempeh, edamame)
- Legumes (lentils, chickpeas, beans, split peas)
- Sprouted legumes
- Quinoa, amaranth, buckwheat
- Nuts (almonds, walnuts, etc.)
- Seeds (pumpkin, sunflower, hemp, chia)
- Algae powders (spirulina or chlorella)
- Nutritional yeast

When choosing protein, look for unprocessed, good-quality options. Try to imagine what your grandparents would have cooked – probably something simple, wholesome and close to its natural form. Real food!

CHOOSE YOUR CARBOHYDRATES WISELY

Not all carbohydrates are created equal. The right ones provide steady fuel for your body, support your brain, and nourish your microbiome with fibre. Refined or highly processed carbohydrates, on the other hand, spike your blood sugars, increase inflammation, damage your gut lining and disrupt your microbiome.

As much as possible, try to only eat the following carbohydrates:

- o Potatoes
- o Sweet potatoes
- o Quinoa
- o Amaranth
- o Buckwheat.

HEALTHY SNACKS AND TREATS

- o Dark chocolate (the real stuff)
- o Boiled eggs
- o Avocado slices
- o Tinned tuna
- o Jerky or biltong
- o Raw veggies
- o Nuts or seeds (soak them first if you have a leaky gut)

EATING OUT TIPS

- o Avoid pasta, bread, or chips, and go for vegetables, a fresh salad, or comforting options like baked or mashed potatoes
- o If you're having a bad day and need some junk food make sure you pair it with a healthy protein or good fat to keep those blood sugars balanced
- o If you're craving pizza, go for a gluten-free or sourdough base
- o If a sandwich is calling your name, try it on sourdough, which is lower in gluten and often better tolerated than regular bread.

Recommended Reading

Rudolph Ballentine – *Radical Healing*

Brené Brown - *Daring Greatly*

Julia Cameron - *The Artist's Way*

Viktor Frankl - *Man's Search for Meaning*

Louise Hay - *Heal Your Body*

Louise Hay - *The Power is Within You*

Louise Hay - *You Can Heal Your Life*

Ryan Holiday - *Stillness is the Key*

Patrick McKeown - *The Breathing Cure*

Emeran Mayer - *The Mind-Gut Connection*

Ohashi - *Reading the Body*

David Perlmutter - *Brain Maker*

David Perlmutter - *Grain Brain*

Margaret Roberts - *My 100 Favourite Herbs*

Eckhart Tolle - *A New Earth*

Eckhart Tolle - *The Power of Now*

Alfred Vogel - *The Nature Doctor*

Alan Watts & Chungliang Al Huang - *The Watercourse Way*

Robb Wolf – *The Paleo Solution: The Original Human Diet*

MY BLOGS

Natural Health Blog – *www.ruthhull.com/blog*
Written for anyone wanting to support their own health naturally, this blog is a gentle guide through holistic living, healing, and nourishment.

Herbs, Healing & Homoeopathy –
https://www.herbhomeopathy.com/
A deeper dive for therapists, students, and anyone curious to explore herbal medicine and homoeopathy more professionally or personally.

About The Author

Ruth Hull is a homoeopathic doctor, herbalist, and counsellor with over two decades of experience in natural healthcare. She holds two master's degrees - one in homoeopathy (health science) and the other in counselling - and has worked with clients around the world, supporting them through fatigue, burnout, and chronic illness.

Alongside her clinical work, Ruth is the author of several widely used health science textbooks. *Drowning Lifeguards* is her sixth book - and her most personal one yet.

She believes that true healing doesn't begin with trying to fix ourselves, but with learning to listen - to our bodies, our stories, and the quiet wisdom within.

Ruth lives in Western Australia with her family and offers one-on-one consultations, group therapy, and practitioner mentoring.

To learn more, visit: www.ruthhull.com

Printed in Dunstable, United Kingdom

70894748R00116